T0135060

Model-Based Approaches to the Internet of Things

Pascal Hirmer

Model-Based Approaches
to the Internet of Things

 Springer

Pascal Hirmer
University of Stuttgart
Stuttgart, Germany

ISBN 978-3-031-18886-2   ISBN 978-3-031-18884-8   (eBook)
https://doi.org/10.1007/978-3-031-18884-8

This Springer imprint is published by the registered company Springer Nature Switzerland AG
The registered company address is: Gewerbestrasse 11, 6330 Cham, Switzerland

For my family, friends, and colleagues.

Preface

Today, the Internet of Things (IoT) is spread throughout many different domains and changes the way we develop software. The uprising of the IoT can be explained by the decrease in hardware costs and the increase in computing power while the physical size of devices decreases over time. Furthermore, new communication technologies and protocols, such as 5G or LoRa, ease the development of highly distributed IoT applications.

In contrast to traditional software systems, IoT applications introduce new challenges regarding their development through highly distributed environments, high heterogeneity, and modular architectures. Furthermore, in the IoT, the focus shifts from only considering software to a focus on the hardware as well. IoT hardware is very heterogeneous and there are many different devices, sensors, and actuators available with very different characteristics and capabilities. In order to develop an IoT application, selecting the right hardware that fits best to the application's requirements suddenly becomes a crucial step.

Overall, we can assume that developing IoT application comes with a high complexity and is much more error-prone than developing traditional software systems. In software development and in computer science in general, models can help in decreasing complexity by providing abstraction and enabling better communication between the different stakeholders involved in development of the application. By first modeling the application's infrastructure, communication, and behavior during execution, potential problems can be detected early and, thus, potentially more robust applications can be developed.

In this book, we introduce how models can be used to describe each step of an IoT application's life cycle, from the hardware selection to the software development, deployment, operation, monitoring, and retirement. We will mostly present our own work regarding these model-based approaches and do not give a general overview of all existing models.

Stuttgart, Germany   Pascal Hirmer
August 2022

Acknowledgements

I would like to thank all colleagues in the AS department of the IPVS, with whom I was always able to have substantive discussions that enriched the results of this book. Furthermore, I would like to thank all the people with whom I was able to write numerous scientific publications as well as the students who supported me in creating prototypes of my concepts. Last but not least, I would like to thank my friends and family who always supported me with a lot of patience.

Contents

1 Introduction 1
    1.1   Motivation 1
    1.2   Structure of the Book 4
    References 5

2 Foundations 7
    2.1   Internet of Things: Introduction and Definitions 7
            2.1.1   Communication in the IoT 9
            2.1.2   IoT Communication: Protocols and Technologies 12
    2.2   Edge and Fog Computing 13
    References 14

3 Scenarios and Challenges 17
    3.1   Scenario 1: Autonomous Transport Vehicles 17
    3.2   Scenario 2: Smart Parking 18
    3.3   Challenges 20
    References 21

4 Life Cycle of an IoT Application 23
    4.1   Step 1: Building the Physical IoT Environment 23
    4.2   Step 2: Modeling the Communication in the IoT Environment 25
    4.3   Step 3: IoT Software Design and Implementation 25
    4.4   Step 4: IoT Software Deployment 26
    4.5   Step 5: IoT Application Execution and Monitoring 28
    4.6   Step 6: IoT Application Adaptation 29
    4.7   Step 7: IoT Application Retirement 29
    4.8   Summary 30
    References 30

5 Model Based Approaches to the Internet of Things 31
    5.1   Selection of Physical IoT Hardware 31
            5.1.1   IoT Toolbox and Building Blocks 32
            5.1.2   Building Block Recommendation and Selection 34

	5.1.3	Related Work	36
5.2		Modeling the Physical IoT Environment	37
	5.2.1	Background	39
	5.2.2	Overview of IoT Environment Models	41
	5.2.3	Model Comparison	56
	5.2.4	Other Surveys	61
	5.2.5	Summary	62
5.3		Setting Up the IoT Environment	63
5.4		Modeling the Communication in the IoT Environment	65
	5.4.1	TDLIoT Requirements	65
	5.4.2	Topic Description Language for the IoT	66
	5.4.3	Related Work	74
	5.4.4	Summary	75
5.5		IoT Software Design and Implementation	76
	5.5.1	Software Building Blocks	77
	5.5.2	Data Processing Model	80
5.6		IoT Software Deployment	82
	5.6.1	TOSCA Foundations	82
	5.6.2	TOSCA and the Internet of Things	84
5.7		IoT Application Execution and Monitoring	87
	5.7.1	Execution and Message Exchange	87
5.8		Monitoring of IoT Applications	89
	5.8.1	Generic Agent Templates	89
	5.8.2	Related Work	94
	5.8.3	Conclusion	96
5.9		IoT Application Adaptation	97
	5.9.1	Used Models	97
	5.9.2	Lifecycle Method for Seamless Integration of IoT Devices .	99
	5.9.3	Related Work	106
	5.9.4	Prototype and Discussion	108
	5.9.5	Conclusion	109
5.10		IoT Application Retirement	109
		References	111

6	**Discussion**	**119**
6.1	Distribution/Decentralization	119
6.2	Heterogeneity	120
6.3	Robustness/Safety	120
6.4	Privacy	121
6.5	Security	121
6.6	Efficiency/Real-Time Capabilities	122
6.7	Energy Consumption	122
	References	122

| **7** | **Conclusion and Summary** .... | **123** |

About the Author

Pascal Hirmer is a post-doctoral researcher at the Institute of Parallel and Distributed Systems of the University of Stuttgart. His research interests include the Internet of Things, distributed data stream processing, software deployment, as well as edge, fog, and cloud computing. His focus lies on data processing and communication in complex IoT environments. Applications for his research include Smart Factories, Smart Cities, and Smart Homes.

Acronyms

The following list comprises the acronyms used in this work in alphabetical order.

API	Application Programming Interface
AWS	Amazon Web Services
BB	Building Block
BBI	Building Block Implementation
BPEL	Business Process Execution Language
BPM	Business Process Management
BPMN	Business Process Model and Notation
BPMS	Business Process Management System
BTLE	Bluetooth Low Energy
CBOR	Concise Binary Object Representation
CEP	Complex Event Processor
CNRS	National Center for Scientific Research
CPU	Central Processing Unit
DDoS	Distributed Denial of Service
DHCP	Dynamic Host Configuration Protocol
CoAP	Constrained Application Protocol
CSAR	Cloud Service Archive
DNS	Domain Name System
ECU	Electronic Control Units
EXI	Efficient XML Interchange
GPIO	General Purpose Input Output
HTTP	Hypertext Transfer Protocol
HVAC	Heating, Ventilation, Air Conditioning
I4.0	Industry 4.0
ID	Identifier
IEC	International Electrotechnical Commission
IESG	Internet Engineering Steering Group
IoT	Internet of Things

IoT ARM	IoT Architectural Reference Mode
IP	Internet Protocol
IT	Information Technology
JSON	JavaScript Object Notation
LAN	Local Area Network
LoRa	Long Range Wide Area Network
LTE	Long-Term Evolution
M2M	Machine-to-Machine
MQTT	Message Queuing Telemetry Transport
NRPE	Nagios Remote Plugin Executor
OASIS	Organization for the Advancement of Structured Information Standards
OCF	Open Connectivity Foundation
OGC	Open Geospatial Consortium
OPC UA	OPC Unified Architecture
OS	Operating System
OWL	Web Ontology Language
QoS	Quality of Service
RAM	Random Access Memory
REST	Representational State Transfer
RFID	Radio-Frequency Identification
RPC	Remote Procedure Call
SenML	Sensor Measurement Lists
SensorML	Sensor Model Language
SLA	Service Level Agreement
SOA	Service-Oriented Architecture
SOAP	Simple Object Access Protocol
SOSA	Sensor, Observation, Sample, and Actuator
SSH	Secure Shell
SSN	Semantic Sensor Network
TCP	Transmission Control Protocol
TDLIoT	Topic Description Language for the Internet of Things
TEDS	Transducer Electronic Data Sheet
TICK	Telegraf InfluxDB Chronograf Kapacitor
TOSCA	Topology and Orchestration Specification for Cloud Applications
TTL	Time to Live
UDDI	Universal Description, Discovery and Integration
UDP	User Datagram Protocol
UPnP	Universal Plug and Play
URL	Uniform Resource Locator
VM	Virtual Machine
W3C	World Wide Web Consortium
WAR	Java Web Archive
WiFi	Wireless Local Area Network

WSDL	Web Service Description Language
WSN	Wireless Sensor Networks
XML	Extensible Markup Language
YAML	Yet Another Markup Language
ZODB	Zope Object Database

Chapter 1
Introduction

1.1 Motivation

> If you think that the Internet has changed your life, think again. The Internet of Things is about to change it all over again!
>
> — Brendan O'Brien

Today, the Internet of Things (IoT) has changed the way we build software systems, enabling a plethora of new applications that are making people's lives easier.

In the Internet of Things, heterogeneous devices are connected through the Internet, using standardized protocols, and communicate with each other to reach common goals [9], such as automating smart homes [5], improving production processes in smart factories [8], or managing traffic in smart cities [3]. An overview of different applications of the IoT is shown in Fig. 1.1. The "game changers" that led to the fast spread of IoT applications were the falling prices of hardware components, the increasing speed, bandwidth, and coverage of wireless networks (e.g., LTE or 5G [1]), and the constantly decreasing size of hardware components that comes with an increase in computing power. All these aspects led to a new way of building software systems consisting of a multitude of small heterogeneous hardware devices able to communicate in a fast and reliable manner.

With the uprising of the IoT, new protocols and hardware components are being developed as well. While WiFi was sufficient in smaller environments, such as Smart Homes, larger scenarios require new ways to communicate. In Smart Cities, for example, the LoRa [2] protocol allows communication over long distances. In Smart and Connected Car scenarios [4], 5G networks offer the required bandwidth and speed to allow cars to communicate with other vehicles in order to warn them of dangerous driving conditions or share traffic information. These new technologies accelerate the spread of IoT applications. Nowadays, the IoT paradigm

© The Author(s), under exclusive license to Springer Nature Switzerland AG 2023
P. Hirmer, *Model-Based Approaches to the Internet of Things*,
https://doi.org/10.1007/978-3-031-18884-8_1

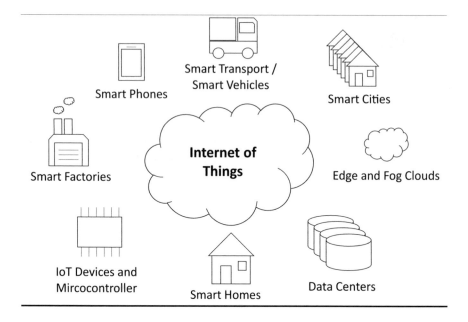

Fig. 1.1 Overview of different applications of the Internet of Things

has reached nearly every domain including factories, healthcare, city management and, of course, our own homes.

With the increase of IoT applications, however, new challenges arise that need to be addressed. Primarily, security and privacy issues grow within IoT applications, since many devices handle sensitive, personal data of their owners. Furthermore, since the communication is mostly wireless, communication channels need to be secured. In recent years, many cases of security issues were uncovered. For example, in 2017, it was discovered that the botnet Persirai was infecting wireless IoT cameras to launch DDoS attacks on web sites [6]. With cheap IoT hardware, security issues are a bigger risk. Unchanged default passwords, easy-to-guess passwords, or a lack of encryption make IoT devices easy targets. Especially in safety-critical scenarios, such as Smart Factories or Smart Cities, security is one of the biggest concerns.

Another issue in IoT applications is privacy. Nowadays, the sensitivity to protect their own data has risen in the population. Especially personal data, such as location, camera footage, or microphone recordings have to be thoroughly protected. Despite these issues, Smart Home devices, such as Amazon Alexa or Google Home, introduce new privacy concerns to people's households. In general, there should not be a tradeoff between sharing private data and the comfort of the services such devices offer. The question who owns the IoT data is, unfortunately, in many cases still unanswered or specific to the laws of different countries.

Besides security and privacy issues, the IoT brings with its advantages new challenges and issues when it comes to data processing. Data is transferred in a highly distributed, decentralized system, which makes monitoring and data processing in general very difficult. To ensure efficient data (pre-)processing and analysis, new technologies are required. In traditional computer systems, data is collected and processed in a central system, to which all data is transferred. However, in distributed systems, this is oftentimes not an option due to high network latency and traffic as well as limited network resources. To cope with this issue, the paradigms of edge and fog computing [10] have been introduced in recent years. While edge computing refers to data preprocessing near to the data sources, e.g., on the IoT devices themselves, fog computing describes a computing layer in between the devices and central computer systems (e.g., in the cloud). In connected car scenarios, for example, the edge layer could be located on the car itself, whereas the fog layer is located at a road-side computing unit.

Finally, energy consumption is an issue that is especially challenging in the Internet of Things. Most devices are usually connected wireless and, thus, do not have a hardwired power source. Since the size of IoT devices is desired to be as small as possible, sizes of attached batteries should be kept as small as possible as well. Hence, energy consumption of IoT devices should be reduced to a minimum. Approaches to achieve this include setting devices into sleep modes and "waking" them up only if they are needed. Especially in the area of Wireless Sensor Networks [7], many different approaches to reduce energy consumption have been introduced in the past.

Overall, Internet of Things systems and applications tend to become very verbose and complex and it becomes difficult to find occurring issues and optimization potentials. Usually, such systems are built ad-hoc and do not follow a proper software-development processes. Furthermore, legacy IoT systems are hardly maintainable and introduce many security and privacy issues.

Figure 1.2 shows an example of an IoT application in a smart factory environment. In this scenario, autonomous transport vehicles—in this case forklifts—transport goods to a truck for delivery. This scenario shows the challenges and opportunities of the Internet of Things. Assuming a full network coverage, transport vehicles can communicate with each other to find optimal paths, avoid collisions

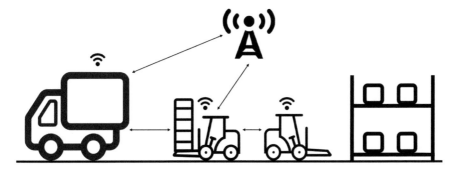

Fig. 1.2 Autonomous vehicles in a smart factory application

and coordinate loading of the truck. In the future, with the upcoming of autonomous driving, even the truck could be operated without a driver. Hence, the whole loading process could be done fully automatically.

However, for this to function properly, the system needs to run in a very robust and reliable manner and the network needs to be stable at all times. Ensuring a reliable operation of complex IoT systems is a great challenge which requires awareness throughout the whole lifecycle of an IoT application.

In this book, model-based approaches are introduced that focus on improving the design, development, deployment, and operation of Internet of Things applications and systems in order to enable reliable, robust, and well-designed IoT applications. We will show how the whole lifecycle of an IoT application can be described using different models, ranging from describing the environment's physical infrastructure, the application logic, including data processing, as well as deployment models and runtime models. A model-based view on IoT application development allows a better understanding of the applications and introducing privacy and security by design, while still ensuring a robust and efficient operation of the applications. The other way around, legacy IoT applications can be transformed into these models to discover different issues, for example, regarding privacy, security, robustness or efficiency.

The book will describe these models in detail and show, based on real-world applications, how they can be applied to complex IoT systems. These applications mostly originate from industry research projects we conducted in collaboration with large manufacturing enterprises. Our scenarios will, for example, include use cases in smart factories, connected cars, and smart cities. These scenarios will, furthermore, be used for validation and evaluation purposes of the introduced models.

1.2   Structure of the Book

In this book, we aim at introducing different kinds of models to build and operate IoT systems and applications. First, we introduce important foundations necessary to understand these models, including, for example, communication paradigms and protocols of the IoT. Second, we start with the beginning of an IoT application's lifecycle by introducing models to design the IoT environment as well as their applications. After the design step, we introduce means to deploy these models and show how the running applications can be monitored and, if necessary, adapted to new requirements or conditions. In the following chapter, we introduce real-world scenarios from industry, showing how our model based approaches can be applied. Finally, we discuss the advantages and limitations of these model-based approaches.

To summarize, here is an overview of the contained chapters.

- **Chapter 1: Introduction** This introductory chapter provides a motivation and a general overview of the topics discussed in this book.

- **Chapter 2: Foundations** Here, different foundations are introduced that are necessary to comprehend the approaches described in this book.
- **Chapter 3: Scenarios and Challenges** In this chapter, two use case scenarios are introduced that serve motivation purposes and will be used throughout the remainder of this book to explain the model based approaches.
- **Chapter 4: Life Cycle of an IoT Application** The life cycle of an IoT application is introduced in this chapter, which is an important foundation for the following model based approaches.
- **Chapter 5: Model Based Approaches to the Internet of Things** This chapter then contains the core content of this book, introducing different models for the different steps in the lifecycle of an IoT application.
- **Chapter 6: Discussion** This chapter discusses the introduced model based approaches based on the challenges described in Chap. 3.
- **Chapter 7: Conclusion and Summary** Here, the findings of this book are concluded. Finally, a summary of the book is given as well as an outlook on future research.

References

1. Ahmad, W., Radzi, N., Samidi, F., Ismail, A., Abdullah, F., Jamaludin, M., & Zakaria, M. (2020). 5G technology: Towards dynamic spectrum sharing using cognitive radio networks. *IEEE Access, 8*, 14460–14488.
2. Bor, M., Vidler, J., & Roedig, U. (). LoRa for the Internet of Things. In *EWSN '16 Proceedings of the 2016 International Conference on Embedded Wireless Systems and Networks* (pp. 361–366)
3. Chourabi, H., Nam, T., Walker, S., Gil-Garcia, J., Mellouli, S., Nahon, K., Pardo, T., & Scholl, H. (2012). Understanding smart cities: An integrative framework. In *2012 45th Hawaii International Conference on System Sciences* (pp. 2289–2297).
4. Coppola, R., & Morisio, M. (2016). Connected car: Technologies, issues, future trends. *ACM Computing Surveys (CSUR), 49*, 1–36.
5. Harper, R. (2006). *Inside the smart home*. Berlin: Springer.
6. Kolias, C., Kambourakis, G., Stavrou, A., & Voas, J. (2017). DDoS in the IoT: Mirai and other botnets. *Computer, 50*, 80–84.
7. Li, J., Ma, H., Li, K., Cui, L., Sun, L., Zhao, Z., & Wang, X. (2018). *Wireless sensor networks*. Berlin: Springer.
8. Lucke, D., Constantinescu, C., & Westkämper, E. (2008). Smart factory-a step towards the next generation of manufacturing. In *Manufacturing Systems and Technologies for the New Frontier* (pp. 115–118).
9. Vermesan, O., & Friess, P. (2013). *Internet of Things: Converging technologies for smart environments and integrated ecosystems*. Denmark: River Publishers.
10. Yousefpour, A., Fung, C., Nguyen, T., Kadiyala, K., Jalali, F., Niakanlahiji, A., Kong, J., & Jue, J. (2019). All one needs to know about fog computing and related edge computing paradigms: A complete survey. *Journal Of Systems Architecture, 98*, 289–330.

Chapter 2
Foundations

2.1 Internet of Things: Introduction and Definitions

The idea of connecting sensors, as it is done in the Internet of Things, has been first introduced by Marc Weiser in 1991 in his book "The Computer for the twenty-first Century" [12]. Weiser used the term "Ubiquitous Computing" for his idea to interconnect different sensors and integrate them in a distributed environment. The term "Internet of Things" has been supposedly introduced later on by Kevin Ashton in 1999 [2]. Combining the original idea of Weiser with the term "Internet of Things" led to our understanding of IoT nowadays.

As the term suggests, in the Internet of Things, so-called "things" communicate through the Internet to reach common goals. Since the term *things* is too abstract, in the scope of this book, we will use the term "device" instead. Hence, in contrast to the field of Wireless Sensor Networks or other IoT definitions, we make a clear distinction between the devices, able to communicate with each other through a network interface, and the sensors and actuators of these devices, being able to monitor or alter the environment.

To make this distinction more clear, we introduce the following definitions as a foundation for this book:

Definition 2.1 We define a **device** of the Internet of Things as a hardware component offering computing capabilities and resources (e.g., CPU, RAM) as well as wireless or wired network interfaces (e.g., LAN, WiFi, Bluetooth, Zigbee, LoRa). A device can be connected to or be embedded with a multitude of different sensors and actuators. A device is capable to connect to the sensors and actuators through hardware interfaces (e.g., GPIO) and run programs to extract, pre-process, interpret and transfer data to other devices or other receiving entities in the Internet (e.g., dashboard applications operated in the cloud).

Furthermore, we distinguish between different kinds of devices since devices can be very heterogeneous and greatly differ in their capabilities:

© The Author(s), under exclusive license to Springer Nature Switzerland AG 2023
P. Hirmer, *Model-Based Approaches to the Internet of Things*,
https://doi.org/10.1007/978-3-031-18884-8_2

Definition 2.2 A **Plug-and-Play Device** is a device that offers easy configuration by just charging them or plugging them to a power source and connecting them to a network. Plug-and-Play devices are mostly used in consumer hardware. With the advantage of easy configuration, however, comes a lack of flexibility with these kinds of devices. More precisely, usually, it is not possible to change the software running on these devices (despite of firmware updates of the manufacturers). Hence, data pre-processing and supported communication protocols are pre-configured on these devices and cannot be changed. Furthermore, sensors and actuators are usually embedded and cannot be changed or extended either. Famous example for plug-and-play devices are radiator or light controls in smart homes.

Definition 2.3 A **Self-Configurable Device** is a device that allows full access to its software and hardware interfaces. Usually, one can connect to these devices through SSH or using hardware interfaces to connect keyboard and monitor. Operating systems and running software of these devices can be fully configured by the user. Furthermore, different kinds of sensors and actuators can be connected through the hardware interfaces of these devices (usually by GPIO). Through scripts, these sensors and actuators can be read and controlled, respectively, and data can be sent and retrieved from other devices or the Internet. While these kinds of devices offer a high degree of flexibility, it also requires expertise in embedded programming, hardware, and network protocols. Famous examples for Self-Configurable Devices are Raspberry Pis, Arduino Boards, or Microcontrollers, such as the ESB8266.

Definition 2.4 The third category of devices we define in the scope of this book are **Gateway-Dependent Devices**. A Gateway-Dependent Device offers very limited computing resources and does not provide any kind of sophisticated (e.g., wireless) communication capabilities. Usually, such devices can connect to sensors and actuators and read their data or send control messages, however, they cannot perform data preprocessing operations or send data to the Internet. Hence, these devices need to be connected to a Gateway, which then handles communication and data transfer. Such a gateway can be, for example, a Self-Configurable Device, such as a Raspberry Pi. Gateway-Dependent Devices include, for example, small micro-controller boards or older versions of the Arduino.

Next, we define the terms Sensor and Actuator and distinguish them to the introduced types of devices.

Definition 2.5 A **Sensor** does not provide any computing or network capabilities. Instead, it needs to be connected to or embedded in one of the above-defined devices. A sensor is capable of measuring certain metrics of the environment, e.g., temperature, humidity, velocity, etc. A sensor can be analog and digital and can be accessed through the hardware interfaces of devices.

Definition 2.6 Similar to a sensor, an **Actuator** does not provide any computing or network capabilities. Instead, it needs to be connected to or embedded in one of the above-defined devices. An actuator is capable of controlling the environment, e.g., by activating switches, turning on radiators or air conditioning systems, or slowing down a car. An actuator can be analog and digital and can be accessed through the hardware interfaces of devices.

Finally, based on these definitions, we define the Internet of Things as follows:

Definition 2.7 In the **Internet of Things**, heterogeneous devices communicate through Internet protocols to reach common goals. Each device can be embedded or attached to various sensors and actuators, which are controlled through their hardware interfaces. An IoT device either provides its own communication interface or is connected through a gateway device.

2.1.1   Communication in the IoT

In this section, we introduce communication paradigms and protocols of the IoT, which are especially important for the approaches introduced in this book. First, we explain the publish-subscribe paradigm and compare it to request-response and, second, we introduce the most important protocols used in the Internet of Things.

2.1.1.1   Publish-Subscribe vs. Request-Response

For exchanging messages in distributed systems, such as the Internet of Things, two communication paradigms have been established: publish-subscribe and request-response. Both paradigms come with different protocols and should be selected based on the requirements of the scenarios. Since communication is an important factor in the IoT, in the following, we introduce both paradigms and explain when they should be chosen.

Publish-Subscribe

The publish-subscribe communication paradigm [5] consists of two entities: (1) the publisher, i.e. the data producer, and (2) one or more subscribers, i.e., the data consumers. Thus, publish-subscribe is used for one-to-many communication. This is especially useful in the IoT, where multiple devices are intended to consume messages from one device, for example, an autonomous vehicle communicating a dangerous situation to the other traffic participants.

Figure 2.1 depicts the structure of a publish-subscribe communication. The central component is a message broker, being responsible for distributing messages to the intended participants. In a first step, the publishers send a message to a so-called *topic*. A topic is a hierarchical path that is used by the subscribers to define which kind of data should be received. Similar to a file path, the topic is

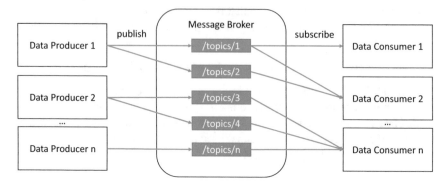

Fig. 2.1 Example of publish-subscribe based communication

usually structured as follows: *<level_1>/<level_2>/.../<level_n>*. In this manner, subscribers can choose to subscribe to all the content available by choosing the root, in this example *level_1*, or by only choosing content from a deeper level in the hierarchy.

For example, a smart home device could publish data from the home under the following paths: *myhome/livingroom/temperature, myhome/livingroom/humidity, myhome/bedroom/temperature,* and *myhome/bedroom/humidity*. In this example, consuming applications can now, for example, choose to subscribe to the whole house by choosing the path *myhome*, only to the bedroom by choosing the path *myhome/bedroom* or only on the temperature of the bed room by choosing the path *myhome/bedroom/temperature*. Furthermore, wild cards can be used to subscribe to all temperature-related messages using the path *myhome/*/temperature* leading to a subscription to the temperature message from the bedroom and living room.

On retrieval of a message from a publisher under a specific topic, the message broker distributes the message to all corresponding subscribers. Usually, message brokers also allow defining which entities are allowed to subscribe as well as security measures, such as encryption and authentication.

In addition, most message brokers allow definition of Quality of Service parameters when publishing a message. Quality of Service parameters allow to define that a message should be delivered at-most-once, exactly-once or at-least-once. In safety critical scenarios, in which message must not be missed, the QoS parameter should be chosen as exactly-once or at-least-once to make sure that no message is lost. However, this will have effects on the performance of the communication. In real-time applications, usually, no QoS parameter is set to ensure a high performance and accepting the potential loss of messages.

A famous example for a protocol realizing publish-subscribe is MQTT, which will be discussed in more detail in Sect. 2.1.2. Famous implementations of the publish-subscribe paradigm are Mosquitto [9], RabbitMQ [4], or Apache Kafka [6]. Many of these implementations are very lightweight and use UDP instead of TPC to ensure a high performance.

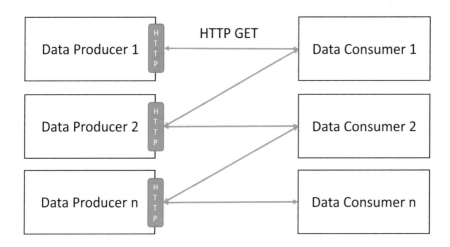

Fig. 2.2 Example of request-response based communication

Request-Response

In contrast to the Publish-Subscribe paradigm, the Request-Response paradigm is focused on 1-to-1 communication and message exchange between two entities. This is depicted in Fig. 2.2. On the one hand, this kind of communication will lead to a significant overhead when sending the same message to several recipients. Furthermore, the address (e.g., URL) of the recipient needs to be known, which is not the case in Publish-Subscribe based communication.

On the other hand, request-response is more robust and secure since the recipients are well-known and, usually, the retrieval of each message is acknowledged by the recipient so the sender can be sure that the message exchange has been successful. Furthermore, it can be made sure that the message does not get delivered to a wrong or unwanted recipient.

Request-Response is usually done using TPC and HTTP, which allows the aforementioned acknowledgements and offers a robust and reliable way of communicating. A message broker or similar middleware components are not required.

Comparison and Recommended Use

Since the two introduced communication paradigms differ in their intended use, some things need to be considered when building IoT systems and choosing the right way to communicate. The first thing to consider is whether the entities of the systems (i.e., devices, cloud services, users) need to know each other. Usually, in the IoT, it is not required that each IoT device knows of the specific addresses, interfaces, or even the existence of the other devices. For example, an autonomous vehicle can publish a message if it recognizes a dangerous situations, such as a hazardous driving conditions, without requiring to know specifics of the other traffic participants, i.e., the consumers of the message.

In other scenarios, using request-response, however, can make more sense, especially if the recipient needs to be a specific entity. For example, if a burglar is detected in a Smart Home, the owner should be notified. In this case, there usually is one recipient and it has to be made sure that the message arrives correctly and completely. In this case, choosing request-response is more feasible since the acknowledgement of the specific message participant is mandatory and it has to be made sure that the correct recipient with the correct unique address receives the message.

Overall, we recommend a mixture of both paradigms in IoT systems, whereas for each communication path, this decision needs to be evaluated separately based on reliability, robustness, and efficiency requirements. While publish-subscribe is usually more efficient, request-response is more stable and secure.

2.1.2 IoT Communication: Protocols and Technologies

In this section, we introduce some established IoT protocols, which will especially be used later on in our scenarios. Note that we rather provide an excerpt of protocols and technologies, we consider especially relevant in the IoT.

The *MQTT* protocol [11] is a very lightweight protocol that enables publish-subscribe based communication. Famous MQTT brokers comprise Mosquitto [9], RabbitMQ [4] or HiveMQ [8]. MQTT is recommended for lightweight IoT applications in which a large amount of smaller messages, e.g., containing sensor values, should be distributed to a larger number of subscribers. MQTT and their corresponding brokers usually use UDP instead of TCP and offer a basic set of Quality of Service parameters to specify whether a message should be delivered, at most once, exactly once or at least once. Furthermore, scalability of the brokers is mostly supported to be employed in larger real-world scenarios. However, with the lightweightness of MQTT usually comes also a reduced robustness, especially when applied to safety critical scenario. For this reason, industry applications tend to use more heavyweight but also more robust systems, such as Apache Kafka [6].

LoRa [3] is a highly sensitive, long-range protocol that allows communication over a long distance using special sender and receiver hardware. LoRa is mostly used in Smart City applications, since the devices need to communicate over long distances, i.e., the whole city. In regard to power consumption, LoRa requires less energy than other communication standards, especially over larger distances. Disadvantages of LoRa comprise a rather low transmission rate and the high costs of the sender and receiver modules.

Bluetooth Low Energy (BTLE) [7] has become the standard for communication in Smart Homes or in communicating with wearables, such as smart watches or fitness trackers. The biggest advantage of BTLE is the very low energy consumption, which, however, also comes with a very short range and a rather unreliable communication. It is very well suited to control smart home appliances or extract data from wearables, however, it is not well suitable for streaming data over longer distances. Here, WiFi (especially WiFi6) mostly has advantages over BTLE that come with a higher energy consumption.

Similar to BTLE, *ZigBee* [13] has become a very well adapted standard for communication in Smart Homes. Its advantages are similar to BTLE the very low energy consumption and offers a longer range than BTLE with 100–300 m line-of-sight. Zigbee however, requires a gateway that provides an ad-hoc network that allows communication between multiple IoT devices within its range. This gateway limits the flexibility in contrast to BTLE, where two devices can communicate with each other directly.

Finally, *5G* [1] networks are the new communication standard for high-bandwith and fast communication, which enables new applications, such as autonomous cars with the need to communicate constantly and transfer a large amount of data. 5G is very reliable, has a large bandwidth and distance and offers many features, such as device discovery and localization. 5G will be the future for communication in Smart Factories and in Connected Car applications, however, it is very costly in terms of licences, senders, and receivers, and, thus, can only be applied in industry scenarios and is not suitable, for example, to be deployed into Smart Homes.

2.2   Edge and Fog Computing

The paradigms of Edge and Fog Computing [10] have become very important, especially in the Internet of Things. Since IoT devices tend to have limited computing resources, data and computing operations need to be transferred to another location, such as a Cloud, to be processed. However, using distant backend clouds, located off-premise is a large issue due to high network latency, which hinders building real-time or even near-real-time applications. For this reason, the paradigms Edge Computing and Fog Computing have been introduced in the past, as shown in Fig. 2.3.

Edge Computing describes computing infrastructure which is located close to the IoT devices that produce data to be processed. So-called *edge devices* need to be located very close to these devices to minimize transport and, thus, network latency. For example, in a smart car, electronic control units (ECU) can be considered as IoT devices that extract data from the car's sensors. A central control unit within the car can then serve as an edge device that is able to aggregate, process, and interpret the data from all ECUs of the car. This edge device should provide sufficient computing power to serve the purpose of the application, for example, to filter data or transform data. Complex data processing, such as data analysis, however, is usually conducted on a more powerful and scalable hardware, which leads to the need for fog and backend cloud environments as well.

Fog Computing can be considered as a layer above the edge devices and provides scalable computing infrastructure, which is still on-premise, however, not as close to the IoT devices as the edge environment. Typically, multiple edge devices communicate with the fog environment and transfer data to be processed

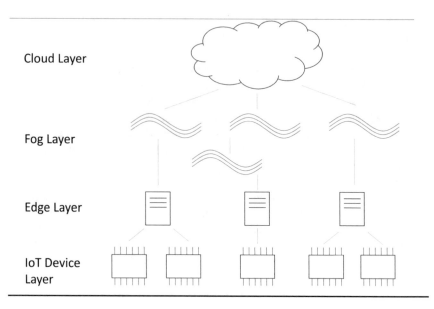

Fig. 2.3 Overview of the different layers in the IoT

or analyzed. For long-term storage, data is transferred from the fog environment to backend clouds. Here, latency and efficiency usually are no issue, since the backend cloud serves more for long-running analysis or for storing historical data in case they are needed in the future.

References

1. Ahmad, W., Radzi, N., Samidi, F., Ismail, A., Abdullah, F., Jamaludin, M., & Zakaria, M. (2020). 5G technology: Towards dynamic spectrum sharing using cognitive radio networks. *IEEE Access, 8*, 14460–14488.
2. Ashton, K. (2009). That 'internet of things' thing. *RFID Journal, 22*, 97–114.
3. Bor, M., Vidler, J., & Roedig, U. (2016). LoRa for the Internet of Things. In *EWSN '16 Proceedings of the 2016 International Conference on Embedded Wireless Systems and Networks* (pp. 361–366).
4. Dossot, D. (2014). RabbitMQ essentials. Birmingham: Packt Publishing Ltd.
5. Eugster, P., Felber, P., Guerraoui, R., & Kermarrec, A. (2003). The many faces of publish/subscribe. *ACM Computing Surveys (CSUR), 35*, 114–131.
6. Garg, N. (2013). *Apache kafka*. Birmingham: Packt Publishing.
7. Heydon, R., & Hunn, N. (2012). Bluetooth low energy. In *CSR Presentation, Bluetooth SIG*. Https://www.Bluetooth.Org/DocMan/handlers/DownloadDoc.Ashx
8. HiveMQ Enterprise, M. Broker. (2016). *MQTT essentials part2: Publish & subscribe*.
9. Mosquitto An Open Source MQTT v3.1/v3.1.1 Broker (online). https://mosquitto.org/
10. Ren, J., Zhang, D., He, S., Zhang, Y., & Li, T. (2019). A survey on end-edge-cloud orchestrated network computing paradigms: Transparent computing, mobile edge computing, fog computing, and cloudlet. *ACM Computing Surveys (CSUR), 52*, 1–36.

11. Soni, D., & Makwana, A. (2017). A survey on MQTT: A protocol of internet of things (IoT). *International Conference on Telecommunication, Power Analysis and Computing Techniques (ICTPACT-2017), 20*, 173–177.
12. Weiser, M. (1999). The Computer for the 21st Century. *SIGMOBILE Mobile Computing and Communications Review, 3*, 3–11. https://doi.org/10.1145/329124.329126
13. Zigbee Alliance Dotdot. (2019). https://zigbeealliance.org/solution/dotdot

Chapter 3
Scenarios and Challenges

3.1 Scenario 1: Autonomous Transport Vehicles

This section presents a case study in a smart factory scenario. We worked on this scenario in cooperation with a large German producer of transport vehicles on shop floors. Our experiences with this scenario helped us with the conception and improvement of our model based approaches for the Internet of Things.

In this scenario, depicted in Fig. 3.1, indoor localization of self-driving vehicles should be realized. These vehicles are able to pick up goods in a warehouse and transport them to a different location. In order to realize this scenario, so it is robust enough for real-world use, it must be known where the vehicles are at all times. For this, each vehicle needs a localization tag, which communicates with multiple stationary tags throughout the factory to determine the current location. Hence, many assets, sensors, and actuators need to be set up. Safety is an essential requirement in this scenario, since human actors are involved as well.

To realize this scenario, first, the physical infrastructure needs to be planned and designed. Firstly, a floor plan of the factory needs to be created, containing all static entities, such as shelves, robots, or machines, that represent an obstacle for the transport vehicles. This floor plan needs to be dynamic, hence, it should be adaptable to a new factory layout. Next, transport vehicles need to be attached with localization tags and an edge device which is able to conduct route planning calculations directly on the vehicle as well as communication with other transport vehicles or central monitoring systems. Next, automated doors need to be attached with receivers and a control unit that enables opening and closing doors on demand by the transport vehicles. Finally, human actors need to be equipped with devices, such as smart phones to interact with the transport vehicles and to the recognizable to avoid possible collisions.

The planning process of the physical IoT environment can become very cumbersome, especially when it comes to selecting suitable technologies that comply with the requirements of the factory owner (in regard to costs, robustness, standard

© The Author(s), under exclusive license to Springer Nature Switzerland AG 2023
P. Hirmer, *Model-Based Approaches to the Internet of Things*,
https://doi.org/10.1007/978-3-031-18884-8_3

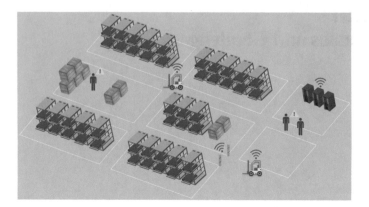

Fig. 3.1 Case study in the smart factory domain (image extracted from [1])

conformity and so on). Here, experts are required that analyze the scenario and recommend the most suitable technologies and protocols to be employed. This planning process, thus, usually requires a lot of time and costs.

In this book, we will introduce a new approach that can ease the selection process of physical IoT hardware and protocols to reduce these planning costs.

After the physical hardware has been planned and selected, the software needs to be implemented, tested, deployed, and monitored, including path planning algorithms, communication channels, monitoring systems, logging systems, and so on. Especially with the high heterogeneity of software systems in the IoT, the process of software creation can become very chaotic, which leads to unstable systems. In the IoT, there is mostly a lack of employing proper standardized software development processes, which is a large issue in safety-critical scenarios. Hence, in this book, we aim at creating models that are able to define the business logic and processes that need to be implemented before starting the implementation. These models can give a proper overview of all involved software components and show how they need to communicate with each other. Through automated software deployment, the implementations following these models can also be directly deployed onto the corresponding infrastructure.

Finally, monitoring is essential, since IoT devices tend to be volatile and failure of IoT devices could jeopardize the operation of the whole IoT system. For this purpose, we introduce a way to annotate the models of the physical environment and the business logic, i.e., the software, to show monitoring information regarding the physical hardware health status and the software health status.

3.2 Scenario 2: Smart Parking

Whereas the first scenario focuses on Smart Factories and Industry 4.0, the second scenario is more focused on Smart Cities, introducing a smart parking applications

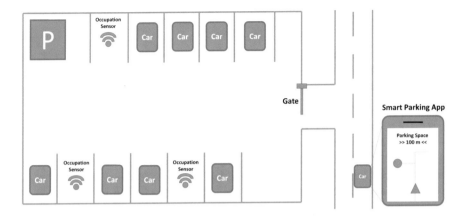

Fig. 3.2 Motivating scenario: smart parking application (based on [2])

that should help drivers of larger cities to find a parking spot in their area. This scenario is depicted in Fig. 3.2.

The IoT devices of this scenario involve parking sensors, which are special sensor that are able to monitor whether a parking space in occupied or not, an edge environment that collects the data of the parking sensors and uses LoRa to communicate with a central cloud server, and the driver's smart phones, which can request data from the cloud server about available parking spots using a smart phone application. Furthermore, electronic gates need to be in place that can be opened by the drivers once they paid for the parking spot.

This scenario is a good example of an application in which devices are on the one hand provided by the IoT application developer, i.e., the provider of the smart parking application, and consumer devices, i.e., the smart phone apps.

To realize such a scenario, requires equipping parking spots with the sensors and setting up an edge cloud environment to collect the data, which could, for example, be on-premise in the parking structure. This edge cloud then comprises a LoRa sender, which sends the information about parking space availability periodically or when something changes. An off-premise cloud environment can then connect through a LoRa receiver to collect the data and store it in a data store. Through an API, the parking spot information can then be collected by the smart phone users in the area. The app is then responsible to filter the parking spaces that are in the area and display them on a map. Once a parking space is selected and paid, a message can be sent through the off-premise cloud environment to the on-premise edge cloud using LoRa, leading to opening the gate to the parking structure.

In this scenario, coping with heterogeneity is an important issue, since different parking space providers use different kinds of sensors, different kinds of communication protocols, data formats, and so on. Hence, this scenario shows that building IoT applications can become very cumbersome, especially when different stakeholders are involved that cannot necessarily be controlled by the application itself.

3.3   Challenges

Based on these scenarios as well as our experience in the Internet of Things, we derive the following challenges to be considered when building IoT applications. Note that these challenges comprise the ones that we consider the most important.

- **Distribution/Decentralization** First, one of the main challenges in the Internet of Things is the high distribution of devices, sensors, actuators, as well as edge, fog, and backend cloud environments. This leads to a decentralized environment that is much harder to control and manage. This includes, for example, a higher complexity in communication, monitoring, or data exchange. Hence, to build reliable and stable IoT systems, it needs to be coped with a high degree of distribution and decentralization.
- **Heterogeneity** Another challenge is the large degree of heterogeneity in the Internet of Things. Not only devices, sensors and actuators differ highly in regard to their capabilities and limitations but also a large variety of communication protocols and paradigms as well as standards exist for the IoT. Thus, it is important that IoT systems are able to combine different kinds of heterogeneous devices, protocols, and standards, which can lead to a cumbersome development process.
- **Robustness/Safety** Especially when it comes to applications in which people could come to harm (e.g., smart cities, autonomous driving), safety is an important issue. Hence, it must be ensured that a failure within an IoT system does not lead to the harm of any involved entity. This challenge is very important but is also very hard to achieve. To ensure safety, different standards and regulations have to be considered throughout the whole development process of the IoT system, including a thorough testing process.
- **Privacy** An important issue is privacy, especially when it comes to sensitive person-related data. There is a high demand for protection and anonymization of personal data, however, in current IoT applications, the privacy aspect is not yet fully considered, which is especially critical if privacy-preserving laws are being violated.
- **Security** In a similar manner, security is an issue that is not only important in IoT applications but becomes more of a challenge since IoT environments are highly distributed and many IoT devices are not equipped with a sufficient degree of security-preserving measures. Hence, it is necessary to ensure security of devices during data transfer as well as for stored data.
- **Efficiency/Real-time Capabilities** In fast-paced scenarios, such as autonomous driving, efficiency and real-time capabilities are important, especially regarding the communication between different IoT devices. New standards and technologies, such as 5G or 6G, must be considered to fulfill the real-time requirements of such scenarios.
- **Energy Consumption** Finally, energy consumption is important to consider since IoT devices are usually wireless and do not possess a hardwired power connection. Thus, there need to be techniques in place to minimize energy

consumption, for example, by putting devices into sleep or standby mode when they are not needed.

References

1. Frigo, M., Hirmer, P., Silva, A., & Thom, L. (2020). A toolbox for the Internet of Things - Easing the setup of IoT applications. In *ER Forum, Demo and Posters 2020 Co-located with 39th International Conference on Conceptual Modeling (ER 2020), Vienna, Austria, November 3–6, 2020* (vol. 2716, pp. 87–100). http://ceur-ws.org/Vol-2716/paper7.pdf
2. Silva, A., Hirmer, P., Breitenbücher, U., Kopp, O., & Mitschang, B. (2018). TDLIoT: A topic description language for the Internet of Things. In *Proceedings of the International Conference on Web Engineering (ICWE)* (pp. 333–348).

Chapter 4
Life Cycle of an IoT Application

4.1 Step 1: Building the Physical IoT Environment

When building an IoT application or IoT system, it is the first step to select, install, and configure the involved physical IoT hardware components. This is also one of the main differences between IoT applications and traditional software systems that are usually not specifically hardware-dependent.

As shown in Fig. 4.1, building the physical IoT environment can be subdivided into three steps: (i) Selection of Physical IoT Harwdare, (ii) Modeling the Physical IoT Environment, and (iii) Setting up the IoT Environment.

Since IoT devices, sensors, and actuators are considered as first-class-citizens in IoT applications, the hardware selection step (i) is of vital importance. The hardware selection process needs to be very thorough since unfitting hardware components can highly decrease functionality and performance of an IoT application. Furthermore, replacement of hardware components after the IoT application has been developed is a great challenge since protocols or other supported technologies vary greatly from device to device and changes can lead to high adaptation costs.

To select hardware components that are fitting the needs of a planned IoT application, a set of requirements need to be established that the hardware needs to fulfill. These requirements usually involve costs, availability, scalability, or robustness of the IoT hardware to be used in the IoT system. Depending on these requirements, it is necessary to analyze and select suitable hardware components, which usually requires experts, which can lead to a costly selection process. Here, workshops involving different stakeholders, i.e., hardware experts, IoT application developers, and so on, are required in which they discuss multiple options and choose one of them together. Only then, clear transparency between the involved stakeholders can be ensured, which is especially important when it comes to larger applications, e.g., in the Internet of Vehicles of Industry 4.0. This whole process can take months without a proper process. In the remainder of this book,

P. Hirmer, *Model-Based Approaches to the Internet of Things*,
https://doi.org/10.1007/978-3-031-18884-8_4

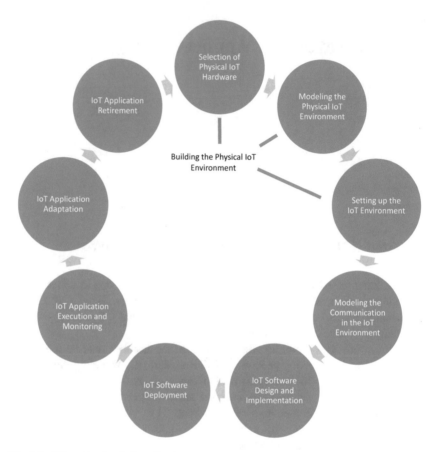

Fig. 4.1 Life cycle of an IoT application

we introduce different model based approaches to ease this process and to make hardware selection more efficient.

After selection of the hardware components, the physical IoT environment needs to be modeled to define how the devices are interconnected and how they should work together to fulfill the needs of the desired IoT application in (ii). A model of the physical environment can help communication between different stakeholders involved in the IoT application and can, thus, lead to a more robust and reliable IoT application. In this book, we will introduce different models to describe IoT hardware environments and we evaluate them based on different criteria.

Finally, the physical hardware components need to be set up and configured in a robust and reliable manner in (iii). In complex scenarios, such as Smart Factories or Smart City production-ready scenarios, this always requires experts. Only in consumer hardware, e.g., in Smart Homes or when using Wearables, such as fitness trackers, non-expert users are usually able to set up and configure their IoT hardware themselves being supported by plug-and-play technology.

However, in the scope of this book, the focus mainly lies on larger IoT scenarios and, hence, we assume that hardware experts are always necessary to set up the IoT environment. Especially in Smart Cities, this could require different kinds of experts that are, e.g., familiar with the electricity grid, radio technology, and so on. Hence, it is necessary to coordinate the hardware setup in a structured manner, introducing standard processes. In the remainder of this book, we will introduce an approach how experts can be supported in setting up complex IoT hardware infrastructures using a toolbox, building blocks, and business processes.

4.2 Step 2: Modeling the Communication in the IoT Environment

After the physical hardware is set up, the next step is modeling the communication of the IoT devices. More precisely, it should be modeled which IoT device provides which functionality, gives access to which data or in which way it can be controlled by overlying applications.

By providing this information, it can be made available which capabilities the IoT environment provides and how they can be accessed to build the desired IoT applications. To realize this, we can consider the IoT devices as services and model their functionalities and access to them similar to service descriptions in Service Oriented Architectures.

For this purpose, we introduce the Topic Description Language for IoT Applications (TDLIoT) in this book. The TDLIoT provides a lightweight description language in which the capabilities and access methods of IoT devices can be defined. To do so, we abstract the devices to so-called topics, where each topic either allows access to data of an IoT device (e.g., sensor data) or to control it or the IoT environment (e.g., by controlling actuators). Quality of Service aspects as well as authentication mechanisms and other characteristics can be defined by the TDLIoT as well.

4.3 Step 3: IoT Software Design and Implementation

After the hardware has been selected and installed and the communication has been modeled, IoT software developers need to design the software based on the capabilities of the hardware, which is even a challenge in traditional software development but becomes especially important in the IoT, since devices tend to be very heterogeneous and limited in their resources and functionality. More precisely, depending on the selection of the hardware, not only different computing resources are available but, furthermore, there might be restrictions, for example, in regard to operating systems, programming languages, or supported protocols or communication technologies to be used. Hence, in contrast to traditional software development, in the IoT, the physical hardware has a big influence in the software development process.

In addition, usually, IoT software is not only installed onto IoT hardware components but is spread throughout an infrastructure of edge, fog, and back-end cloud environments which require different kinds of software development approaches. For example, to ensure scalability of software modules in a backend cloud environment, the software should be developed in a stateless manner.

Another issue here is that software developers that were trained in traditional software development oftentimes do not have the specific skill-set to work in IoT application development, immediately. Hence, when it comes to introducing IoT projects and applications into a company, additional training could be required how to develop software for these largely distributed and limited IoT devices, including new programming languages, communication protocols, newly arising standards, and so on.

In the scope of this book, we introduce different approaches that can potentially ease software development, especially when it comes to non-expert IoT software developers. Approaches include, for example, modular or service based architectures, in which applications can be built based on a given toolbox, which shall reduce the effort and costs in IoT application development.

4.4   Step 4: IoT Software Deployment

After the software components have been implemented for all devices, edge, fog, and backend cloud environments, they need to be deployed onto the physical environment. In complex scenarios, this could mean deploying software on hundreds or even thousands of IoT devices, which is a cumbersome and costly task if conducted manually. For this reason, automated software deployment tools and standards are used, such as the Topology and Orchestration Specification for Cloud Applications (TOSCA) [2]. Using overlying models (e.g., topology models of TOSCA) that describe which software component needs to be deployed onto which hardware component enables better planning and a more robust automated deployment.

Figure 4.2 shows an example based on the TOSCA standard.[1] On the left, an abstract example is shown how such deployment models could look like in general, and on the right, an exemplary initialization of such a model is shown.

The left of Fig. 4.2 shows how the typical structure of such a model looks like. Usually, IoT applications are connected to each other, some of them running on embedded devices, others running on Edge, Fog, and Backend Cloud environments.

---

[1] Note that this figure shows a simplified TOSCA model by omitting deployment and implementation artifacts or corresponding policies to improve the readability.

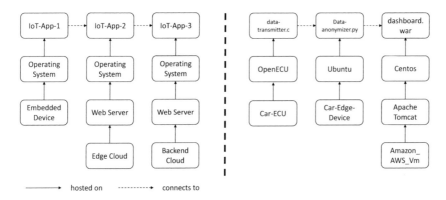

Fig. 4.2 TOSCA based example of a deployment model

On the top, the application components are modeled. To improve readability, we assume a simple example in which each application is contained in a single model, however, in reality, models tend to become more complex. The next layer then comprises platform components, such as operating systems or web servers. Finally, on the bottom, i.e., the leaf nodes of the TOSCA model, hardware components should be modeled to define on which infrastructure the software module should be deployed. This is vital when it comes to deployment models suitable for the IoT. The relation *hosted on* defines the way components are hosted onto each other and *connects to* defines which components communicate with each other.

The right of Fig. 4.2 shows an exemplary instantiation of this generic model. Let us assume that a car should make its data (current speed, location, etc.) available in a dashboard. To enable this, three software modules are required. First, the *data-transmitter*, implemented in C, should be deployed on the car's Electronical Control Unit (ECU), which runs the operating system OpenECU, which can be seen in the left stack. In the middle stack, a module is provided in Python that anonymizes the typically privacy-sensitive data produced by the car. We can assume that an edge device is available in the car, which runs the operating system Ubuntu and the anonymization component should be run onto this OS. Finally, a dashboard application is implemented in Java and packaged as a Java Web Archive (WAR), which is then hosted onto the Java Application Server Apache Tomcat which runs on the OS Centos. Finally, the OS is running inside a virtual machine hosted by Amazon AWS. The *connects to* relations finally show how the data flows in this example. This model can then be used for automated deployment of the involved software components throughout the entire IoT infrastructure.

We will introduce different possibilities for deployment using the TOSCA standard in Sect. 5.6. However, when it comes to deployment onto highly embedded devices, e.g., within a car, there is still a lack of standards and corresponding tools and manual deployment steps are usually inevitable. We will discuss these issues in the remainder of this book.

4.5 Step 5: IoT Application Execution and Monitoring

After the deployment step, the software required for the IoT application should be up and running. However, when it comes to execution and operation of IoT applications, communication between the modules plays an important role in these highly decentralized and distributed environments. To enable reliable operation of these applications, we need standard protocols as well as a uniform message exchange. Otherwise, maintaining such an environment can become very cumbersome and costly, especially if interfaces and message formats change. Regarding execution and operation of IoT applications, we introduce ways to model how the different involved devices and software components are able to communicate, and we discuss monitoring and adaptation of these applications.

Monitoring is of vital importance in the IoT, since IoT applications are heavily distributed systems, which are usually volatile and susceptible to hardware or software failures. Hence, it is necessary to introduce a comprehensive monitoring of software and hardware components of the IoT application. Here, centralized or decentralized monitoring systems could be used, depending on the requirements of the scenario. Centralized monitoring systems are easier to manage and provide a single interface to users, however, they are less efficient and provide a single-point-of-failure. In contrast, decentralized monitoring is more complex to manage, since each component is monitored individually and the monitoring information needs to be collected and processed to be suitable for human users.

Famous examples of monitoring systems include Nagios[2] and the TICK stack[3] (as shown in Fig. 4.3), which enable centralized monitoring, which is the typical

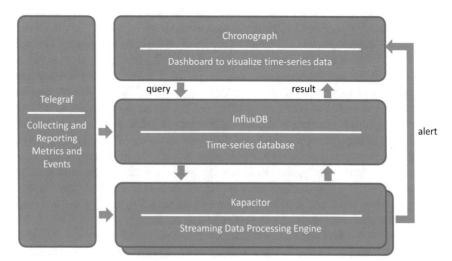

Fig. 4.3 Architecture of the TICK stack (based on [1])

---

[2] Nagios Monitoring System: https://www.nagios.org/.

[3] TICK Stack: https://www.influxdata.com/.

approach. In the TICK stack, which has become some sort of de-facto standard for monitoring, different software components work together to enable monitoring data extraction and transfer (Telegraf), storage (InfluxDB), monitoring and alerting (Kapacitor) and visualization (Chronograf).

However, even though the TICK stack is an approved and established means to monitoring, when it comes to real-time reaction on issues, distributed monitoring approaches are important as well. Monitoring will not be the main focus of this book, however, we will show how established monitoring systems fit into the introduced models and can be deployed and operated together with the IoT applications.

4.6 Step 6: IoT Application Adaptation

As it is the case for software and hardware systems in general, updates and adaptations are necessary in the lifecycle of an application, either to fix bugs and issues or to add new functionalities. However, software updates tend to be very complex in distributed IoT applications, especially when they should be done online, i.e., while the application is still running.

For this, automated software deployment tools and standards, such as the ones described in the deployment step, are necessary. Furthermore, since adaptations influence each step of the lifecycle process, it is necessary that involved models are very dynamic in the sense that they can be adapted and reused easily, without any larger downtimes of the application. The earlier an adaptation happens in the lifecycle of an IoT applications, the bigger the influence on the whole application. If an update or replacement of hardware components occurs, re-testing and deployment of applications is usually unavoidable, which can become costly if the involved models are too static and inflexible. Hence, the need for adaptations in the early steps of the lifecycle should be reduced to a minimum which only works if the steps are properly planned. Furthermore, in case of failing devices, IoT applications should be able to adapt to the new condition without failing completely.

In the scope of this book, we will should how we can adapt some of the introduced models according to new conditions or requirements.

4.7 Step 7: IoT Application Retirement

The final step of our lifecycle is the retirement of the IoT application once it reaches its lifetime either because it is not needed anymore or it is replaced by a newer application. In this case, software needs to be undeployed and the hardware needs to be uninstalled and removed from the environment. The models created during the lifecycle of the IoT applications can help in understanding which software and hardware to uninstall and which components could be reused in future applications.

Furthermore, the models can help in setting up similar applications in the future. If shared among different IoT software developers, software development effort can be reduced greatly since oftentimes different IoT applications can still be very similar, for example, when applied to a different domain. Also, in some cases, only part of an IoT application should be retired and other parts should still be kept running, especially in larger and more complex applications. In this case, the models can be adapted by removing the unnecessary hardware and software components, which leads to corresponding undeployment and uninstalling steps.

Overall, we build on these introduced steps in this book and we show how they can be conducted more effectively by the use of different models. Note that we omit the software testing step, which is of course a crucial and essential step before software deployment, however, we consider IoT software testing out of scope in this book and refer to the work of Sand et al. [3].

4.8   Summary

The introduced life cycle method is required for each IoT application being created and covers each step necessary to operate the application from the design phase to deployment, execution, monitoring, and retirement.

Of course, legacy applications, that have not been built according to the models introduced in our lifecycle, are considered as well. In this case, these legacy applications start at the software execution and monitoring step of the lifecycle. In case of any adaptation, the lifecycle continues in the described order.

For existing applications, it could make sense to create the models, for example, describing the physical infrastructure, even though the application was already built, in order to increase maintainability and to improve documentation of the legacy application. The details of the model based approaches in each step of the introduced lifecycle are described in the next chapter.

References

1. Juggery, L (2018). Architecture of the TICK Stack. Online, https://betterprogramming.pub/the-tick-stack-as-a-docker-application-package-1d0d6b869211
2. OASIS Topology and Orchestration Specification for Cloud Applications. (2013). Advancing open standards for the information society. http://docs.oasis-open.org/tosca/TOSCA/v1.0/os/TOSCA-v1.0-os.pdf
3. Sand, B. (2016). IoT testing - The big challenge why, what and how. In *Internet of Things. IoT Infrastructures* (pp. 70–76)

Chapter 5
Model Based Approaches to the Internet of Things

The first step of the lifecycle is building the physical IoT environment. As described in the previous Chap. 4, we are dividing this step into three substeps. First, the physical IoT hardware needs to be selected for a planned IoT application based on a set of requirements. Second, once the physical IoT hardware has been selected, the whole physical hardware environment needs to be modeled, describing how the selected hardware devices interact and how they are connected to each other. Third, the environment needs to be set up by technical experts. In the selection process of physical IoT hardware, a toolbox can assist in selecting components that fit the requirements of the planned IoT application, which is described in the following.

5.1 Selection of Physical IoT Hardware

When building IoT applications, it first needs to be decided which physical hardware should be used for achieving its desired goals. Choosing the best fitting hardware is a very important step, since exchanging hardware after the software has been developed is very difficult and leads to cumbersome and costly adaptations in the application software. Hence, it is important to support IoT application developers in choosing the right IoT hardware for their application and its specific requirements.

To do so, we describe the *IoT Toolbox* as introduced by Frigo et al. [1], which consists of a set of building blocks, each representing a specific IoT hardware component, which could be, for example, a device, a sensor, an actuator, a specific network technology (e.g., sender or receiver), and so on. The idea is that, based on a set of requirements, the toolbox is able to make recommendations for hardware components to be used for the IoT application. These requirements could, for example, originate from workshops involving all important stakeholders that are involved in creating the IoT application. Requirements could, for example, include costs, efficiency, security, privacy, or existing know how with specific hardware.

P. Hirmer, *Model-Based Approaches to the Internet of Things*, https://doi.org/10.1007/978-3-031-18884-8_5

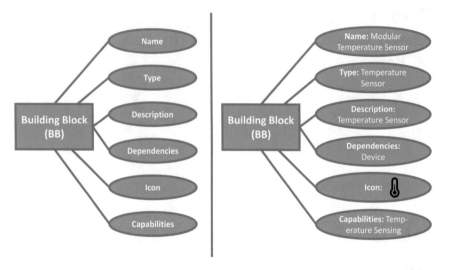

Fig. 5.1 Left: Remainder of a building block; Right: Building block example for a temperature sensor (based on Frigo et al. [1])

In the following section, we first introduce the IoT Toolbox and its including building blocks. Then, once the hardware components are selected, we introduce different models that can be used to describe how they are interconnected and how they fit together within one larger environment. After that, we show how technical experts and non-technical domain experts can be supported in setting up an IoT environment using a business process oriented approach.

5.1.1   IoT Toolbox and Building Blocks

As mentioned before, the IoT toolbox offers a set of building blocks (BB) that are divided into different categories. These categories include different hardware components, which can assist domain experts in the first step of our lifecycle method, i.e., the IoT hardware component selection process. By connecting different building blocks using pre-defined requirements and capabilities, it can be ensured that the hardware components fit to the requirements of the IoT application to avoid any future issues in the application's development process.

Figure 5.1 depicts on the left the structure of a building block. Each block contains a name, a type, a description (suitable for domain experts), dependencies to other building blocks, an icon to ensure recognition, and a set of capabilities that are able to fulfill the applications' requirements. On the right of Fig. 5.1, an example building block is given for a modular temperature sensor. In an initial phase, experts of the specific IoT domain need to agree upon a common list of building blocks, which has to be extensible, since new technologies appear frequently in the IoT.

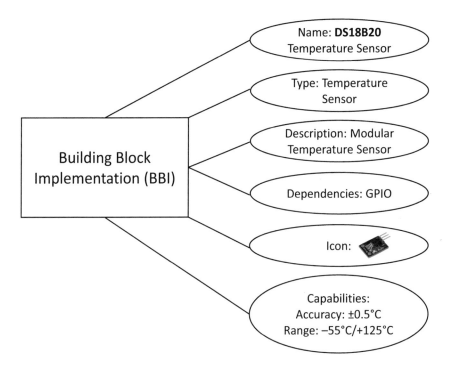

Fig. 5.2 Building block implementation example for a temperature sensor (based on Frigo et al. [1])

We are aware that this is an ambitious goal, which would require some sort of standardization IoT experts agree upon. In the vision of the IoT toolbox, IoT technology providers create building blocks themselves in order to promote their new solutions and add them to the toolbox. With a strong community, the toolbox could grow to a comprehensive collection of all kinds of IoT components.

Each BB has one or more implementations attached to it, which are referred to as building block implementation (BBI) in the following. These BBIs are concrete instantiations of a BB. That is, a BBI represents a concrete hardware component. Furthermore, BBIs can have a set of dependencies that could require installation of different BBIs. For example, some BBIs might require the installation of a specific power line or need to be attached to another device to work. For example, a simple temperature sensor without its own power source would need to be attached to a more powerful device, such as a Raspberry Pi.

An exemplary Building Block Implementation for the Temperature Building Block is shown in Fig. 5.2. As can be seen, it provides specific metrics and capabilities of the hardware component. In this example, capabilities are the accuracy and range of the sensor. Based on the application's requirements, the toolbox can suggest suitable IoT hardware components based on the BBI's capabilities.

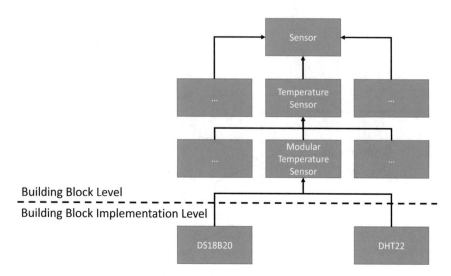

Fig. 5.3 Hierarchy of building blocks, example for a temperature sensor (based on Frigo et al. [1])

For our BB example in Fig. 5.2, implementations could include different modular temperature sensors, such as the DS18B20, DHT22, or AM2320. Once domain experts decide upon the need for temperature sensing in the IoT application, they will find the according building block in the toolbox and will be able to select one of the corresponding building block implementations.

BBs and BBIs can be defined in a hierarchical structure, meaning that building blocks can inherit characteristics of other building blocks, enabling their specialization. The depth of the hierarchy is arbitrary and is decided by the designer of the toolbox. Figure 5.3 depicts an example of hierarchical building blocks using a temperature sensor. In this example, as a root, a very generic building block "Sensor" is defined, representing all possible kinds of sensors. This BB is then derived to the "Temperature Sensor" building block, which represents all temperature sensors. This BB can then be derived once again, for example, to Modular Temperature Sensors, represented by a corresponding BB. In our example, this BB then has two different implementations (in this example DS18B20 and DHT22).

5.1.2 Building Block Recommendation and Selection

After the toolbox is filled with building blocks and their corresponding building block implementations, IoT application developers, i.e., the domain experts and different involved stakeholders, need to define a set of requirements for their application's hardware. These requirements need to consider different aspects, such as costs, accuracy, efficiency, security, privacy, available computer resources, and so on. Defining such requirements usually requires involving different stakeholders and technical experts for each of these areas. Hence, we recommend predefining a fixed set of requirements the domain experts can choose from, which eases requirement definition and the matching of the requirements to BBs in a later step.

Based on the resulting set of requirements, BBs and BBIs can be selected. The matching could be done by the domain experts themselves, by browsing the toolbox and finding the building blocks with suitable capabilities, or automatically, by matching requirements and capabilities and making recommendations. In any case, the toolbox gives a good overview regarding which technologies and approaches are available for IoT applications without the need for domain experts to acquire this knowledge themselves.

Now, let us assume that a domain expert aims at developing a smart parking application in a smart city as introduced in Sect. 3.2. The goal of this application is that drivers can find available parking spots near their location. Sensing whether a parking space is available or not should be conducted by cheap sensors, since many of them will be required, for instance, one sensor per parking lot. Sensor data should be aggregated by gateways and should be sent to a cloud application, which is accessed by the mobile devices to check parking space availability. The gateways should be distributed at strategic positions in the city to achieve maximal coverage. Since parking spaces are distributed among the whole city, long range communication is necessary. Hence, the gateways serve as receivers for a long-range protocol. This scenario would lead, for example, to some of the following requirements:

- Sensing requirements

  - R1: Parking Space Occupation
  - R2: Low costs

- Communication requirements

  - R3: Long-range communication

- …

In a next step, browsing the toolbox could retrieve the following BBs and corresponding BBIs from which domain experts can then choose:

- Sensing

  - BB-1: Occupancy Sensor (fulfills R1, R2)

    · BBI-1.1: Occupancy sensor module HC-SR501
    · BBI-1.2: Occupancy sensor module EKMB1301111K

- Communication

  - BB-2: LORA sender (fulfills R3)

           · BBI-2.1: RFM95 LoRa Module—868 MHz
           · BBI-2.2: Dragino LoRa Shield—868 MHz
           · requires BB-3: LORA receiver

     – BB-3: LORA receiver (fulfills R3)

           · BBI-3.1 LoRa Click with RN2483
           · BBI-3.2 Lora Sx1276 Wireless Receiver 868 MHz Module E32-868t20d
           · requires BB-2: LORA sender

- ...

As shown in this example, found BBs and their respective BBIs can have additional dependencies, which leads to the need for other BBs/BBIs. In this case, the LORA sender requires an according receiver and vice versa. In this manner, depending BBs can be retrieved in the selection process as well.

This example illustrates how requirements and building blocks fit together. After the set of BBs and BBIs is retrieved from the toolbox, the domain experts and their involved stakeholders need to choose from the BBIs the most fitting ones. This decision is usually made, for example, based on the hardware costs or available expertise handling this specific kind of hardware.

Now that the required hardware components have been selected using the IoT toolbox, it needs to be modeled how they fit together, i.e., how they are interconnected and how the devices are distributed among the IoT environment, which can be described using so-called IoT environment models. These are introduced in Sect. 5.2, comparing different existing models based on different criteria.

5.1.3 Related Work

In recent years, similar model based approaches to the toolbox approach of Frigo et al. [1] have been developed that are discussed in the following.

Franco da Silva et al. [2] present "Internet of Things Out-of-the-Box", an approach using the OASIS standard TOSCA [3] to set up IoT environments. In their work, the goals are similar to ours, setting up IoT environments with as less effort as possible. Instead of a toolbox, they are using a TOSCA Type Repository, however, the steps of defining requirements and selecting the most suitable TOSCA types are not described. Furthermore, the processes they use for setting up the IoT environments do not support human tasks. Consequently, hardware devices and other steps that have to be conducted manually should already be set up in their approach.

Yelamarthi et al. [4] introduce a modular IoT architecture. Their work is similar to the building block approach since they use modular building blocks to create an IoT architecture. Their work shows that IoT architectures work best when they are built in a modular manner since replacing parts of the architecture becomes more easy. We built on the idea of such a modular architecture and extend it by providing a means to set it up through a holistic lifecycle method based on our toolbox containing a variety of building blocks.

In the past, many IoT environment models have been developed. These models contain information about the devices of the IoT environment, their properties (e.g., location or computing resources), the attached sensors and actuators, and their interconnection. However, these models highly differ in their content, the formats being used, and the domain they are applied to. Famous examples for such models are SensorML [9] or IoT-Lite [5, 7]. Some of these models are developed and maintained by large organizations, others have been created in research projects and are maintained by a small group of people. Furthermore, some of them are even standardized. These models can be used to provide a standardized mean to describe the building blocks we aim for. Since many models are built based on ontologies (e.g., using the Web Ontology Language OWL [10]), important aspects, such as hierarchies and inheritance, dependencies, and attributes, are already provided. In the following chapter, some of these models are described in more detail.

5.2 Modeling the Physical IoT Environment

As described in the previous section, the first step in the life cycle of an IoT application is selecting the required hardware components, including all IoT devices, sensors, actuators, and so on. The hardware selection process can be done by the use of the introduced IoT Toolbox. This selected infrastructure then serves as the foundation to implement the IoT application's software. After the hardware has been selected, it needs to be defined how they interact with each other and how they will be connected. Planning the IoT infrastructure is a very crucial step since the hardware plays an essential role in the application's performance. Models can assist IoT application developers into designing the whole physical environment before setting it up. A thorough design process, involving different stakeholders, is a crucial step because exchanging hardware components of a fully implemented and running IoT application requires a lot of adaptation effort and, thus, could lead to high costs and downtimes of the application.

In the following, we refer to models that describe the physical infrastructure of an IoT application as *IoT environment models*. These models offer a way to design an IoT application and share this model for discussion with different involved stakeholder to make sure that the hardware environment fulfills all requirements of the planned IoT application.

In previous work [11], we conducted a comprehensive survey, investigating different kinds of models focusing on physical IoT environments. In the following, the results of this survey are summarized and we give a conclusion, which of them can be most suitable for the Internet of Things. Note that nowadays many new models and standards are developed and hence, the list of models should be extended in the future.

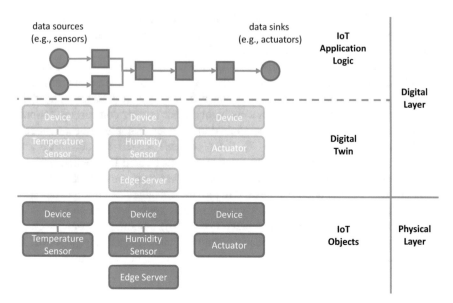

Fig. 5.4 Layers of the internet of things (based on [11])

Before diving into the different kinds of models that exist to model a physical IoT environment, we first need to categorize different aspects of the plethora of existing models [12]. We divide these aspects into two main layers as shown in Fig. 5.4: the physical layer and the digital layer.

While the physical layer of an IoT environment describes aspects of IoT hardware objects (e.g., devices, sensors, and actuators) and their connections, the digital layer represents the so-called *digital twin*,[1] which is a program that either mirrors or simulates a physical device [13, 14]. The digital twin, hence, refers to aspects that describe ongoing services provided within an IoT environment. Finally, on the top layer, the IoT application logic refers to models that logically use the services provided by the digital twin to achieve the goals of an IoT application, e.g., monitoring HVAC systems in a Smart Home.

When analyzing existing IoT environment models, we found out that they vary widely in their content, formats, and the domain to which they are applied. We found many examples of such models, including SensorML [9], IoT-Lite [5], IEEE 1451.2, OPC UA, and many more.

We further found out that some of these models are created, standardized and maintained by large organizations or companies while other models were created by university researchers in the scope of specific IoT research projects and, thus, are only maintained by a small group of people having a limited scope and reachability.

---

[1] oftentimes also referred to as digital shadow or digital mirror.

To support IoT application developers to find a suitable model to describe the physical environment of their IoT applications and to provide other researchers with an overview of existing IoT environment models, we will describe the most promising models and rate them according to different criteria. Note that we consider not only standards, but also new approaches that are not yet fully mature. Once a model is selected, it can then be used to describe the IoT hardware environment.

5.2.1 Background

Before we can describe the different models, some foundational background is necessary to mention, including environment models in general as well as ontology models, since most of the presented models build on ontologies using different standards, such as, for example, OWL2.[2]

5.2.1.1 Internet of Things and Their Environment Models

As discussed in Chap. 4, in the first step of the lifecycle of IoT applications, models can support building the physical environment with its devices, sensors, actuators, senders, receivers, and so on. As mentioned before, we refer to these kinds of models as *IoT Environment Models*.

We define an IoT environment model based on previous work [15] as follows: an IoT environment model contains representations of (i) devices, sensors, and actuators of the IoT environment and (ii) the connections among them. In order to define which devices, sensors, actuators, communication protocols, or data formats are contained within an IoT environment, a large amount of models were developed that aim at a standardized description of such complex environments. However, these models differ greatly regarding the abstraction level, focus, or genericity. For example, some models focus on the network; others focus on the physical characteristics of the devices. In addition, some models describe the characteristics of the environment itself (e.g., a smart factory) and others do not.

For IoT application developers, these models can be very helpful to understand the structure of the IoT environment or even be used as an underlying data model for their applications. However, choosing the right model for a specific application is a difficult task. The wrong decision could lead to a *vendor lock-in*, because changing the underlying data model of an application is error-prone and time-consuming.

---

[2] OWL2 Specification Document: https://www.w3.org/TR/owl2-overview/.

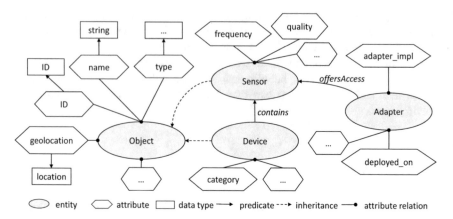

entity   attribute   data type → predicate --→ inheritance ——• attribute relation

Fig. 5.5 Example of an ontology-based model for IoT environments based on [17] and extracted from [11]

5.2.1.2 Ontology Models

Ontologies are an important concept in the scope of IoT environment models. Ontologies offer a possibility to describe semantics between entities, leading to large, semantic graphs. Each entity usually has relations of the type *subject (S)*, *predicate (P)*, and *object (O)*. Through these relations, semantics can be expressed [16]. For example, the IoT device *Raspberry Pi* (the subject) is *located* (the predicate) in *room B* (the object). Furthermore, the subject *Raspberry Pi (S)* could be *connected* (P) to an *Arduino board (O)*. A famous language to create ontologies is the Web Ontology Language 2 (OWL 2).

Especially for the IoT, using ontology models makes sense because a device is highly interconnected with other devices and with its surroundings. For example, a device can be located in a room of a building, is attached with sensors and actuators, and has connections to other devices. Using the already in place graph model of ontologies enables a means to describe such dependencies in an easy manner. Consequently, many of the developed models mentioned in this article are based on ontology models to describe IoT environments.

Figure 5.5 shows an example ontology schema for the IoT. In this model, sensors and devices are entities derived from a generic *Object* entity. Each device contains sensors, and each sensor is connected to an adapter, which provides access to it. Actuators are omitted in this simple example. This example shows how ontology models can be used in order to describe IoT environments. Many models introduced in this survey are similar to this example.

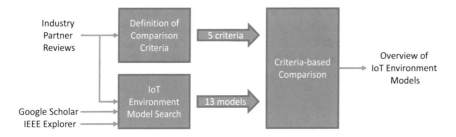

Fig. 5.6 Research methodology (based on Franco da Silva et al. [11])

5.2.2   Overview of IoT Environment Models

With this background in mind, we describe different IoT environment models based on our previous work [11]. By doing so, we analyze different models that focus on the different layers of an IoT environment, as shown in Fig. 5.4.

Now, to conduct the survey, we used a specific research methodology as depicted in Fig. 5.6. This methodology is comprised of three main steps: (i) definition of comparison criteria based on Internet research as well as Industry partner reviews, (ii) we search models according to given keywords in the Internet of by suggestion of Industry partners, and (iii) we compare these models according to the criteria.

In the first step, we define five criteria covering important characteristics of IoT models. These criteria were identified from experience and interviews in the scope of the German industry projects SmartOrchestra [18] and Industrial Communication for Factories (IC4F) [19]. These and similar projects we have been involved in, have many industry partners with expertise in the IoT and Industry 4.0 domains.

Afterwards, we searched for models in two different databases by using combinations of the following keywords: "*IoT*", "*Internet of Things*", "*environment model*", and "*ontology*". The following search string was used: "*(("Internet of Things environment model" OR "IoT environment model") OR ("Internet of Things ontology" OR "IoT ontology"))*". Papers that were found by the search string were selected or excluded based on their title, abstract, and full-text reading. We excluded papers without accessible full-texts in the selected databases, not written in English, or that were not peer reviewed. Papers that did not have the focus on modeling any aspect of IoT environments based on their paper title or abstract were also excluded. Furthermore, models that showed dependencies on specific technologies (e.g., ZigBee) or systems (e.g., IoT platforms) were excluded as well.

Moreover, we also took into consideration models that were referred to by industry partners. In the last step, the resulting thirteen models were compared based on the defined criteria. The criteria and criteria-based comparison are presented in Sect. 5.2.3. The publication period of the compared models ranges from 1998 to 2019.

With these keywords, we were able to find a plethora of different IoT environment models, which we will describe in the following. Please note that these models tend to be very comprehensive and we will not provide all their details. However, we will focus on the most important aspects relevant to model IoT applications as aimed for in this book. Overall, we want enable a broad overview and comparison in order to support the choice of a suitable model for IoT application developers to conduct the first step of our lifecycle method.

5.2.2.1 HomeML

The first model we describe is HomeML, which is an XML-based open format for the data exchange focusing exclusively on smart home environments. HomeML was first proposed by Nugent et al. [20]. The HomeML XML format enables the description of a smart home, including its rooms and the sensors within the rooms. Actuators and network communication are not considered by this model. Consequently, HomeML focuses on the physical layer, e.g., the devices (cf. Fig. 5.4). With the focus on Smart Homes, HomeML does not provide much flexibility, however, with the possibility to create a graphical model as well, it can be more suitable for smaller scenarios as Smart Home scenarios usually are.

The main concept in HomeML are device descriptions that cover different aspects, for example, the device ID, location, and type, and as a description of different events generated by the device. We show an XML example of HomeML in the following, which is based on McDonald et al. and Nugent et al. [20, 21].

```xml
<?xml version="1.0" encoding="UTF-8"?>
<homeML>
 <inhabitantDetails>
  <inhabitantID>454542</inhabitantID>
 </inhabitantDetails>
 <location>
  <locationID>4754</locationID>
  <locationDescription>Living
   Room</location
   Description>
  <locationDevice>
   <ldeviceID>454584</ldeviceID>
   <deviceType>Temp Sensor</deviceType>
   <units>Celsius<units>
   <deviceDescription>Temperature Sensor
   Living Room </deviceDescription>
   <deviceLocation>
    <xPos>10.5</xPos>
    <yPos>12.3</yPos>
    <zPos>54.2</zPos>
   </deviceLocation>
   <event>
    <eventID>1</eventID>
```

```
      <timeStamp>11:20:50, 9/24/11</timeStamp>
      <data>23.1</data>
    </event>
    <event>
     <eventID>2</eventID>
     <timeStamp>11:21:44, 9/24/11</timeStamp>
     <data>23.2</data>
    </event>
   </locationDevice>
  </location>
 </homeML>
```

In this example, HomeML XML is used to model a simple Smart Home scenario. First, inhabitants can be modeled, which are people owning or controlling the devices of the smart home. Each inhabitant can be clearly identified by a unique ID.

Next, a location is described, which has an ID and a description, in this case the Living Room. Within a location, an arbitrary amount of devices can be contained. Each device, again, contains an ID and a description, however, it also contains a type, measurement units, a location using X, Y, and Z axis, and a number of events that can occur. An event has an ID, a timestamp when it occurs, as well as corresponding data. In our example, a temperature sensor is modeled that measures the temperature of the living room.

This example shows how the structure of an HomeML XML document can look like. This structure can be used to define Smart Home scenarios and can, furthermore, be used for 3D visualization tools of the environment to improve communication between different stakeholders.

Since it can be cumbersome to write XML, the modeling tool homeML suite was introduced by McDonald et al. [21]. A new and extended version of homeML (Version 2.2) was introduced in 2013. As mentioned before, homeML is specialized for smart homes and does not aim at being a generic model for the IoT.

5.2.2.2 IEEE 1451.2

The second model that we discovered is the IEEE 1451.2 standard, which is part of a group of IEEE standards aiming to ease connectivity of sensors and actuators [22, 23]. In IEEE 1451.2 a so-called transducer electronic data sheet (TEDS) needs to be specified that allows for self-description of transducers, which, in other words, are sensors or actuators. The transducer electronic data sheet is stored in a nonvolatile memory and contains, e.g., the type, operation, and calibration of a sensor or actuator. In Table 5.1, an example of a TEDS for a voltage sensor provided by the manufacturer Futek [24] is shown.

As can be seen in this example, the TEDS defines, in a very detailed level which kind of sensor is involved, which kinds of values it is able measure, as well as many characteristics, such as response times, calibration dates, power supply infos, and

Table 5.1 Exemplary transducer electronic data sheet (TEDS) of a voltage sensor (based on [24] and extracted from [11])

TEDS structure	Property	Value	Units
Basic TEDS (64 bits)	Manufacturer ID	Futek Advanced Sensor Technology, Inc.	–
	Model number	MP	–
	Version letter	P	–
	Version number	300	–
	Serial number	123456	–
TEDS template: high-level voltage output (154–253 bits)	Template ID	30	–
	Physical measurand (units)	psi	–
	Minimum physical value	0	psi
	Maximum physical value	50	psi
	Transducer electrical signal type	Voltage sensor	–
	Full-scale electrical value precision	0–10 V	–
	Minimum voltage output	0	V
	Maximum voltage output	10	V
	Mapping method	Linear	–
	AC or DC coupling	DC	–
	Sensor output impedance	1	Ohms
	Response time	0.001	s
	Excitation/power requirements	Power supply/excitation source	–
	Power supply level, nominal	24	V
	Power supply level, minimum	14	V
	Power supply level, maximum	30	V
	Power supply type	DC	–
	Maximum current at nominal power level	0.001	A
	Calibration date	11/3/2016	–
	Calibration initials	NWH	–
	Calibration period	365	days
	Measurement location ID	1	–
User data	–	–	

so on. As can be seen here, TEDS is focusing on the physical level and describes sensors and actuators. Hence, it is recommended to combine TEDS with other models so describe larger environments. Recently, the IEEE 1451.2 standard has been adapted to the IEEE standard 21450 [25].

IEEE 1451.2 and 21450 aim to provide generic models for the IoT and are very comprehensive. As an IEEE standard, these models have to be reviewed and approved by an independent expert committee. As a consequence, these standards can be adopted by companies in order to realize complex IoT applications. An important issue when it comes to standards is whether they have been implemented or not. For IEEE1451.2 and 21450, implementations have been developed by

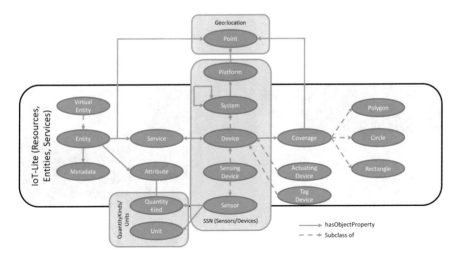

Fig. 5.7 IoT-Lite ontology (based on [29], relation labels omitted for better overview)

Conway et al. [26] and by Song and Lee [27]. In addition, Cherian et al. [28] employed this standard to connect industrial legacy sensors to Ethernet networks.

5.2.2.3 IoT-Lite

As mentioned before, many of the models are based on ontologies, which is especially useful in the IoT where highly distributed and interconnected environments need to be modeled. One of these ontology based models is IoT-Lite.

The IoT-Lite ontology [5, 29] has been developed in the scope of the European funded projects FIWARE (https://www.fiware.org) and FIESTA-IoT (http://fiesta-iot.eu). IoT-Lite aims at being a lightweight instantiation of the Semantic Sensor Network (SSN) ontology, which is a widely used ontology model for sensor networks. Its goal is to represent resources, entities, and services in heterogeneous IoT platforms.

The structure of an IoT-Lite ontology model can be seen in Fig. 5.7. Here, IoT devices cannot be modeled directly but rather need to be sub-classified as sensing devices, actuating devices, and tag devices, which is a passive device, such as a radio-frequency identification (RFID) tag.

Apart from these different kinds of devices, different other entities can be defined, including (i) *Entity* which is basically any entity or service in the IoT environment, (ii) *System*, which is basically an abstraction for the sensing and actuating infrastructure, and (iii) *Services*, which provide the functionality of IoT devices. IoT-Lite is under submission as a standard at the World Wide Web Consortium (W3C) organization, where several implementation examples of the ontology are provided, but still needs to be approved to become a full standard.

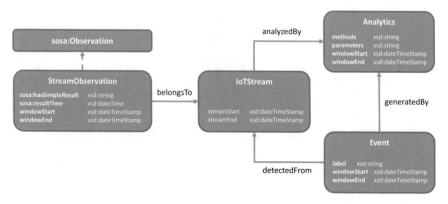

Fig. 5.8 IoT-Stream ontology (based on Elsaleh et al. [30])

Overall, IoT-Lite is a very useful model, since it is very generic and, furthermore, aims at reducing the complexity of other IoT models by describing only the main IoT concepts. However, despite being generic, IoT-Lite can be easily extended to represent IoT concepts also in detail and in different domains. Regarding the layers shown in Fig. 5.4, IoT ranges through all layers since it can describe physical components as well as IoT application components.

5.2.2.4 IoT-Stream Ontology

Another ontology based model is the IoT-Stream ontology [30, 31], which is a lightweight model focusing on IoT data streams generated within IoT environments. The data streams can be semantically annotated to give them a specific meaning. The IoT-Stream ontology model, similar to IoT-Lite extends the SSN ontology and its lightweight core including the types Sensor, Observation, Sample, and Actuator (SOSA) [48].

Figure 5.8 shows the structure of the IoT-Stream ontology. As can be seen, the focus lies on the data to be processed in different manners. The StreamObservation element defines the window of a data stream, which is time-based and has a clear start and end timestamp. The IoTStream has a number of StreamObservation elements belonging to it and connects the streams to analytics tasks. The stream itself consists of a number of events that also have a start and end timestamp.

The IoT-Stream information model focuses on modeling stream observations and their analysis and events that are detected from it, which are captured in four classes: *IotStream*, *StreamObservation*, *Analyticsprocess*, and *Event* classes. IoT-Stream includes modules for annotation, consumption, and querying of data. In addition, different tools are included that facilitate the use of semantics in IoT. Regarding the layers of Fig. 5.4, IoT-Stream focuses exclusively on the IoT application logic layer.

5.2.2.5 IoT Architectural Reference Model (IoT ARM)

The IoT Architectural Reference Model (IoT ARM) [52] is another ontology based model that was developed in the European Lighthouse project IoT-A.[3] IoT ARM consists of several sub-models that address architecture specific characteristics for the IoT. Its primary model is the IoT Domain Model, which describes the main concepts of the IoT (e.g., devices, services, virtual entities) and the relations among them. The IoT ARM model supports the modeling of users and their interaction with physical entities in the physical world. A physical entity is represented in the digital world by a virtual counterpart called the virtual entity.

Figure 5.9 shows an exemplary instantiation of the model, in which a humidity and temperature sensor are connected to a device, which triggers an alarm as soon as these values exceed a certain threshold. A connected Android App is then capable of subscribing to these alarm events to find a solution to the occurring problem. As can be seen, IoT ARM offers a means to model different entities of different layers, including the physical hardware entities as well as the virtual applications. In IoT-ARM, different sensors can be attached to an device. The distinction between device and sensor is not done by most other standards and enables a more fine-grained modeling of the environment.

In conclusion, IoT ARM focuses not only on the physical layer but also on the digital twin and the application specific components.

5.2.2.6 Open Connectivity Foundation (OCF)

The Open Connectivity Foundation (OCF) IoT Management and Control specification enables standardized device and service descriptions for the management and control of IoT environments using Universal Plug and Play (UPnP) technology [32]. One of its main goals is to describe sensors and actuators of UPnP and non-UPnP networks as well. Hence, it considers network characteristics, as well as physical characteristics. It also provides a means to define general-purpose devices that are connected to sensors and actuators.

Figure 5.10 shows how the OCF framework looks like. On top, there are the different stakeholders that aim at building applications based on the framework, including consumers, enterprise, industrial stakeholders, and so on. These stakeholders are represented by Profiles in the OFC that use the Core Framework.

The Core Framework itself provides means for discovery, provisioning and communication of services as well as a Resource Model for RESTful interaction, which is the focus on our survey. They also support different protocols for messaging, as shown on the bottom of Fig. 5.10.

A reference implementation of the OCF specification has been developed in the IoTivity project [34]. OCF IoT Management and Control is generic and does not

---

[3] https://cordis.europa.eu/project/id/257521.

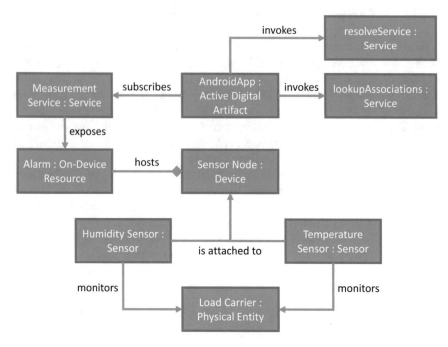

Fig. 5.9 IoT-ARM example instantiation (based on Bauer et al. [52])

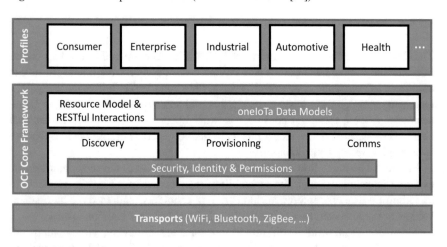

Fig. 5.10 OCF architecture overview [33]

focus on a specific IoT domain; hence, it can be applied to different use cases and applications. Furthermore, it describes the physical layer, as well as the digital twin layer depicted in Fig. 5.4.

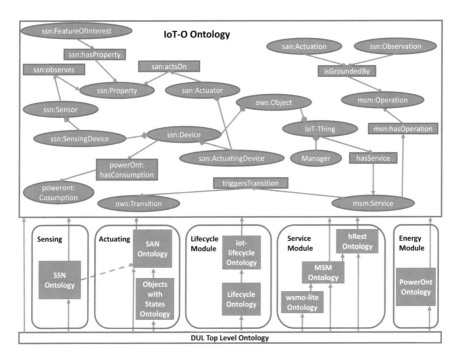

Fig. 5.11 IoT-O ontology overview (based on Seydoux et al. [35])

5.2.2.7   IoT-O

IoT-O is an ontology proposed by Alaya et al. [36] and Seydoux et al. [35]. IoT-O extends the oneM2M standard to support semantic data interoperability. IoT-O handles the sensing, actuating, and service concepts of M2M devices. In order to cover all relevant IoT concepts, it comprises a set of existing ontologies, i.e., DUL (Dolce-UltraLite), SSN, SAN, QUDV, OWL-TIME, and MSM ontologies, which were selected to describe five main concepts: sensor, observation, actuator, actuation, and services models.

As shown in Fig. 5.11, IoT-O is very comprehensive and is based on different top-level ontologies. It uses different ontologies and combines their strengths to form a very widely applicable ontology model. For sensing, the SSN ontology is used, for acting SAN, Lifecycle ontology for lifecycle management, MSM, hRest, and wsmo-lite for service definition, and PowerOnt as a means to define power consumption. This leads to a very powerful ontology model, combining all these different ontologies into one.

IoT-O is currently not a standard, and no reference implementation could be found. It is generic and enables a wide range of use case scenarios in different IoT domains. IoT-O also enables description throughout all layers of the IoT (cf. Fig. 5.4).

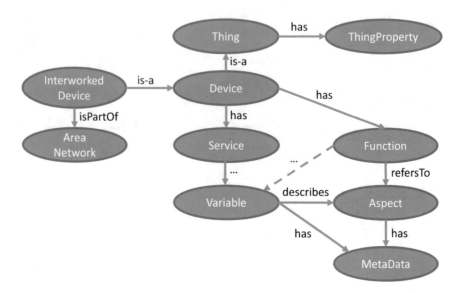

Fig. 5.12 OneM2M ontology (based on Li et al. [38])

5.2.2.8   oneM2M Base Ontology

The oneM2M base ontology [37] is an IoT standard that specifies the semantics of the data handled in the oneM2M specification. This ontology defines a device as a derivation of a generic *thing* designed to accomplish a particular task through functions of the device. These functions are exposed in the network as services of the device.

As shown in Fig. 5.12, in the OneM2M ontology, the top level element is a Thing, which stands for a specific Device. A Device can contain Services or Functions with different Variables, Aspects, or Meta Data. Furthermore, Devices can be interconnected through an Area Network.

In the context of oneM2M, a device is assumed to be always capable of communicating via a network. Furthermore, sensors and actuators are abstracted as devices, whose concrete functionalities can be expressed as services. Thus, sensors and actuators are implicitly represented via their services. In conclusion, the oneM2M base ontology describes the physical and digital twin layers.

5.2.2.9   OPC UA Information Model

The OPC UA Information Model (IEC 62541-5) [39] belongs to the OPC Unified Architecture (OPC UA) standard, which focuses on the interoperable, secure, and reliable exchange of data in the scope of industrial communication. It guarantees, therefore, platform independence and seamless flows of information among devices

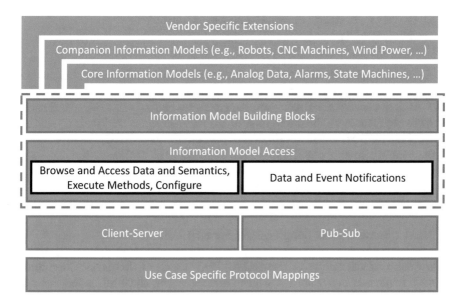

Vendor Specific Extensions

Companion Information Models (e.g., Robots, CNC Machines, Wind Power, ...)

Core Information Models (e.g., Analog Data, Alarms, State Machines, ...)

Information Model Building Blocks

Information Model Access

| Browse and Access Data and Semantics, Execute Methods, Configure | Data and Event Notifications |

Client-Server | Pub-Sub

Use Case Specific Protocol Mappings

Fig. 5.13 UA architecture overview (based on [41])

from multiple vendors. OPC UA defines a client-server communication paradigm, in which an OPC UA server provides access to data and functions structured as defined by the OPC UA Information Model. OPC UA clients can then interact with the information model through standardized services [40]. The overall architecture of the Unified Architecture is shown in Fig. 5.13.

An open-source implementation of OPC UA in the programming language C is *open62541* (https://open62541.org). OPC UA focuses mostly on the digital twin layer, i.e., the services and interfaces of the IoT devices, but also enables the description of the physical layer, i.e., the IoT devices, sensors, and actuators.

5.2.2.10 Sensor Measurement Lists (SenML)

Sensor Measurement Lists (SenML) is an IETF Internet draft specification for media types to represent measurements and device parameters [42]. SenML provides a common data model to describe measurements and simple metadata about measurements and devices, which can be represented in JavaScript Object Notation (JSON), Concise Binary Object Representation (CBOR), eXtensible Markup Language (XML), and Efficient XML Interchange (EXI). In this model, the data are structured as a single array containing so-called *SenML records*. Each record contains fields, such as the sensor's unique identifier, the measurement time, value, and unit. An example of a temperature sensor measurement in the JSON syntax is shown in the following.

```
[ { "n": "urn:dev:ow:10e2073a01080063",
"u": "Cel",
"v": 23.1 } ]
```

In this example, the array has a single record, in which the sensor measures the value 23.1°C. However, SenML does not provide a model to describe an entire IoT environment with its resources, connections, and services. Hence, SenML exclusively focuses on the description of the physical layer. SenML is a standard (RFC 8428 [43]) of the Internet Engineering Steering Group (IESG) and is primarily prominent in scientific publications, such as by Su et al. [44] or by Kaivonen and Ngai [134]. A reference implementation of SenML is provided on the open-source platform GitHub (https://github.com/core-wg/senml-spec).

5.2.2.11   Sensor Model Language (SensorML)

The Sensor Model Language (SensorML) [9] is an Open Geospatial Consortium (OGC) implementation standard, which provides models and XML schema encoding to define processes and processing components involved in measurements and the transformation of observations. Its focus lies on the process of measurement and observation; however, it also provides a means to define the physical characteristics and capabilities of sensors and actuators. Components, such as sensors and actuators, are modeled as physical processes, which can accept one or more inputs and produce one or more outputs. The structure of SensorML is shown in Fig. 5.14. SensorML also supports the linking between processes and, thus, the concept of process chains or workflows. Hence, SensorML is able to describe all layers of the IoT (cf. Fig. 5.4).

SensorML is generic; however, the focus lies on physical processes, interconnecting sensed data with actions. Besides the XML representation, an ontology model for SensorML is provided online (http://www.sensorml.com/ontologies.html). In the following, a minimalist example of how a sensor can be described in SensorML is provided.

```
<sml:PhysicalComponent gml:id="temperature_sensor" ... >
<gml:description>Temperature sensor</gml:description>
<gml:identifier codeSpace="uid">1</gml:identifier>

<!-- Observed Property = Output -->
<sml:outputs>
<sml:OutputList>
<sml:output name="temp">
<swe:Quantity definition=
 "http://sweet.jpl.nasa.gov/2.2/quanTemperature
 .owl#Temperature">
<swe:label>Air Temperature</swe:label>
<swe:uom code="Cel"/>
</swe:Quantity>
```

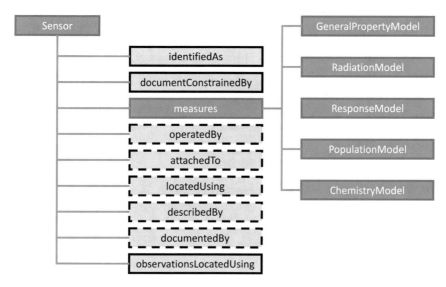

Fig. 5.14 SensorML structure (based on McKee [45])

```
</sml:output>
</sml:OutputList>
</sml:outputs>

<!-- Sensor Location -->
<sml:position>
<gml:Point gml:id="stationLocation"
srsName="http://www.opengis.net/def/crs/EPSG/0/4326">
<gml:coordinates>47.8 88.56</gml:coordinates>
</gml:Point>
</sml:position>
</sml:PhysicalComponent>
```

In this example, a temperature sensor is modeled as a physical component, containing a description and a unique identifier. The measurements of a sensor are described by the element *sml:outputs*, while the element *sml:position* corresponds to the location of the sensor.

In SensorML, the output of the sensors is the focus. Hence, one can define a list of outputs containing the unit and the concrete definition of the measurement, in this case provided by a reference to another ontology.

Furthermore, the location of the sensor can be defined using different means. In the example, this is done by point coordinates.

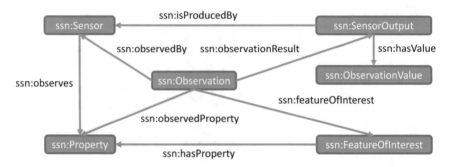

Fig. 5.15 SSN overview (based on Souleiman et al. [47])

5.2.2.12   SSN Ontology

The SSN ontology is an OWL 2 ontology to describe sensors and observations, which was developed by the W3C Semantic Sensor Network Incubator group (SSN_XG) [46]. Being a W3C standard, currently, SSN is a widely used ontology, which serves as a basis for many other ontology models, e.g., IoT-Lite [7], IoT-O [36], or the ontology model introduced by Hirmer et al. [17].

The SSN ontology [8], as shown in Fig. 5.15 describes sensors with respect to their capabilities, measurement processes, observations, and deployments. It applies the Stimulus-Sensor-Observation (SSO) ontology design pattern to describe the relationships between sensors, stimulus, and observations. SSN provides a good foundation to be extended in order to fit specific use cases. Furthermore, SSN mostly focuses on the physical layer and the digital twin layer. Last year, Janowicz et al. [48] introduced the Sensor, Observation, Sample, and Actuator (SOSA) ontology, which acts as a replacement of SSN's core ontology (SSO). The SOSA ontology is lightweight and general-purpose and models interactions among observations, actuation, and sampling. SOSA resulted in the process of rethinking the SSN ontology based on changes in scope and target audience, technical developments, and lessons learned.

5.2.2.13   Vorto

Eclipse Vorto [50] is an IoT open-source development infrastructure for the creation and management of agnostic, abstract device descriptions. A simple language is provided in which devices (e.g., a fitness band) and their functionality (e.g., heart rate monitor and step counter) can be described. These descriptions are then published as information models in a centralized Vorto repository. Since Vorto is provided with a comprehensive programming language, all layers of the IoT can be described.

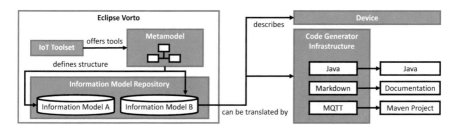

Fig. 5.16 Eclipse Vorto architecture (based on [49])

As shown in Fig. 5.16, the Vorto framework is distributed among different components. First, the Eclipse Vorto core component is run centrally, for example, in a backend cloud. It consists of an IoT Tool Set, providing different means to access devices, sensors, and actuators, a metamodel describing the structure of the IoT environment, as well as Information Models, describing the concrete physical environment.

On the devices themselves, an agent is running that can be implemented in different programming langues, e.g., Java. The code can even be generated by Vorto's information models. The agent itself is responsible to extract sensor data or control actuators and to connect to the Vorto core component to provide it with these information.

Vorto is an implementation focused approach, which provides several tools to create device descriptions. It aims at a practical approach to describe devices so that they can be directly used for application development. As part of the Eclipse Foundation, Vorto has been developed as open-source and is available on GitHub (https://github.com/eclipse/vorto).

5.2.2.14 Model Categorization

Figure 5.17 depicts an overview of all aforementioned IoT models and on which aspects of the IoT layers they focus. This figure refers to Fig. 5.4, which shows the different layers of the IoT, the physical layer, including IoT objects, and the digital layer, including the digital twin, as well as the IoT application logic. As shown in Fig. 5.17, most of the investigated models cover the physical layer, as well as the digital twin. Some models, i.e., homeML, IEEE 1451.2, and SenML, only focus on the physical layer. Other models cover all layers, e.g., IoT-O or SensorML, whereas only IoT-Stream focuses on the IoT application logic only. However, since IoT-Stream is an extension of SSN/SOSA, other layers could be modeled as well. Which model to choose highly depends on the requirements of the specific use case they should be applied and over which layers these requirements spread.

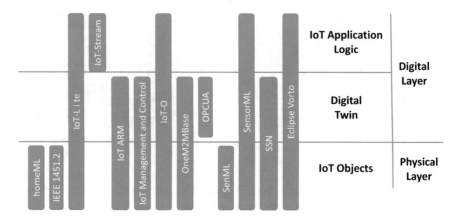

Fig. 5.17 IoT models mapped on layers of the internet of things (based on Franco da Silva et al. [11])

5.2.3   Model Comparison

As shown in our research methodology, we derived different comparison criteria from Internet research as well as interviews with industry partners. As a result, we provide five criteria covering the most important characteristics of the IoT Environment Models. The criteria we identified are: ❶ maturity, ❷ support of hierarchies, ❸ availability and community support, ❹ implementation, and ❺ geolocation support.

The criteria-based comparison of the IoT environment models are summarized in Table 5.2. In the following, we explain how the models were rated based on the different criteria.

5.2.3.1   Criterion ❶: Maturity (Standard/Non-Standard)

The first criterion specifies the maturity of the models, for example whether a model is an approved standard of an organization, such as OASIS, W3C, or OGC, or not. We assume that a standard that was approved by such organizations went under a thorough reviewing process and, thus, has been checked for feasibility. Furthermore, we assume that a standard has an advantage in contrast to, for example, a work that was published in scientific papers and might have not yet been properly validated or used in real scenarios. Consequently, maturity is an important factor for the evaluation of IoT environment models.

homeML is an academic approach proposed as a collaboration work of the universities of Ulters and Luleå. The *IoT-O* ontology is an academic collaboration of the National Center for Scientific Research (CNRS) and the university of Toulose. It is not a standard, but uses the oneM2M standard as a basis and extends it.

Table 5.2 Criteria-based comparison. ❶: Maturity, ❷: hierarchy, ❸: availability, ❹: implementation, ❺: geolocation. Models marked with * were suggested by industry partners (based on Franco da Silva et al. [11])

Model	❶	❷	❸	❹	❺	Year	Remarks
homeML	non-standard	✗	✗	✗	✓	2007	Designed for smart homes [20, 21]
IEEE 1451.2*	standard	✗	✓	✓	✗	1998	Focuses on sensors [22, 23, 25]
IoT ARM	non-standard	✓	✗	✗	✓	2013	Generic reference model [52]
IoT-Lite	submitted	✓	✓	✓	✓	2016	Uses SSN ontology [5, 7, 29]
IoT-Stream	non-standard	✓	✓	✓	✓	2019	Uses SSN ontology [30, 31]
IoT MC*	standard	✓	✓	✓	✗	2013	Also known as IoTivity [32, 34]
IoT-O	standard ext.	✓	✗	✗	✗	2015	Uses SSN ontology [36]
oneM2M base	standard	✓	✓	✓	✓	2018	Focuses on services of IoT devices [37]
OPC UA*	standard	✓	✓	✓	✗	2016	Established in smart factories [39, 40]
SenML*	standard	✗	✓	✓	✓	2012	Focus on sensors and sensor values [42, 43]
SensorML	standard	✗	✓	✓	✓	2014	Supports processes [9]
SSN	standard	✓	✓	✓	✓	2005	Well-established IoT ontology [8, 48]
Vorto*	non-standard	✗	✓	✓	✗	2017	Provided as programming language [50]

Furthermore, *IoT ARM* was developed within a European Lighthouse research project. *IoT-Stream* is not a standard; however, it is very mature, including a detailed documentation and a corresponding implementation.

In contrast to the aforementioned models, several models are approved standards by well-known organizations: *IEEE 1451.2 and 21450* are standards by the IEEE organization; *IoT Management and Control* is a standard by the Open Connectivity Foundation (OCF); *OPC UA* is a standard by the International Electrotechnical Commission (IEC); *SensorML* is an Open Geospatial Consortium (OGC) implementation standard; and the *SSN* ontology is a standard by the W3C Semantic Sensor Network group; furthermore, the *oneM2M base* ontology is a published specification to the oneM2M organization, while *SenML* is a standard by the Internet Engineering Steering Group (IESG). The *IoT-Lite* ontology is currently in submission at the W3C organization.

Finally, *Vorto* is not a standard, but is an open-source tool that has been supported and developed by the Eclipse Foundation.

5.2.3.2   Criterion ❷: Support of Hierarchies

Representation of hierarchies is an important factor when modeling environments in the IoT, since they normally contain hierarchical deployments among the different existing IoT objects. There are two main types of hierarchies, *grouping* and *abstraction*. For example, through grouping, it should be possible to model complex systems, such as production machines in a smart factory, which contain a high amount of devices, sensors, and actuators. This enables group-based querying. Such relations can be of vital importance, for example, when conducting monitoring for predictive maintenance [51]. Furthermore, through abstraction, generic types can be defined. For example, different sensor modules measuring temperature can be derived from the generic type *temperature sensor*. Consequently, we investigate whether some support of hierarchies can be expressed in the IoT environment models. For example, an ontology-based model supports natively both mentioned types of hierarchies. Other models normally need to provide such a means separately.

With respect to the surveyed models, many of them do not distinguish among device, sensor, and actuator, i.e., sensors and actuators are abstracted as a device, a thing, or a system, which has specific functionalities for sensing or acting. In this case, we analyze whether hierarchies can be built among devices, things, or systems. If a model provides concepts for grouping, it is indicated in our evaluation.

The first version of *homeML* provides a two level deep hierarchy: A *smart home* must contain at least one *room*, and a room can contain zero or more *devices*. Hierarchies among devices cannot be modeled. Furthermore, devices can be grouped by rooms, i.e., a group of devices existing in a specific room. In the latest version of homeML (Version 2.2), the described hierarchy and grouping are, with minor changes, still kept.

The *IoT-Lite* and *SSN* ontologies define a device as a *system*, which can be a *subsystem* of other systems, enabling in this way hierarchical relations among devices. Similarly, the *IoT-O* ontology defines a device as a *thing*, which can consist of other things, enabling in this way hierarchical relations as well. Since *IoT-Stream* builds on SSN/SOSA, it also supports hierarchical relations. The *oneM2M base* ontology defines a *device*, which can consist of other devices, also enabling hierarchical relations.

The *OPC UA Information Model* defines an *AddressSpace*, which contains *Nodes* that can be organized hierarchically or by grouping. The *IoT ARM* abstracts sensors and actuators as devices; however, it is possible to build hierarchies among devices. Furthermore, groups can be modeled as well.

Finally, IEEE 1451.2 describes only one device at once, i.e., no hierarchy or groups can be modeled. Similarly, *SenML*, *SensorML*, and *Vorto* do not support the description of hierarchies.

5.2.3.3 Criterion ❸: Availability and Community Support

The third criterion specifies whether the model is publicly available or not and, furthermore, if a wide community is involved in its future development. Clearly, a large community of users and developers, or a larger organization, is required in order to establish and to further develop an IoT environment model. To realize this, the model should either be available open-source, or, if it is closed-source, it should be developed and used by a larger organization.

For *homeML*, a simple link to the XML schema was provided by Nugent et al. [20]; however, the link is not working. No schema could be found for *IoT ARM*; however, there are many UML diagram examples in several related publications [52]. The

IoT-O ontology is also not available online; the authors only provide a figure of their model.

The *IEEE 1451.2* and *IEEE 21450* standards, *W3C IoT-Lite*, *IoT-Stream*, *OCF IoT Management and Control*, the *oneM2M base* ontology, *OGC SensorML*, and the *SSN_XG SSN* ontology are available online by their corresponding organizations. The *OPC UA Information Model* is available to download upon registration on the OPC Foundation website. Furthermore, the *SenML* specification is available as an Internet draft on the IETF organization website. Finally, *Eclipse Vorto* is available open-source, providing tool support to create information models.

5.2.3.4   Criterion ❹: Implementation

The fourth criterion specifies whether an implementation for the IoT environment models exists. In scientific papers, for example, interesting concepts are created that, however, might not have a corresponding implementation. For the usage in real scenarios we aim for in this article, an available implementation is of vital importance. This also includes available tools for model creation and management. For models without a corresponding implementation, we discuss whether an implementation could be realized.

For almost every surveyed model, there are implementations or examples. Only for *homeML*, *IoT ARM*, and *IoT-O*, no implementations were found. A web address to the homeML suite was provided by McDonald et al. [21]; however, the address is not accessible. An implementation of IoT-O is not available as well.

An implementation of the *IEEE 1451.2* for sensors with a web address was provided by Wobschall et al. [53]. Furthermore, several implementation examples of the *IoT-Lite* ontology are provided in the submitted document in the W3C organization. *IoT-Stream* provides an implementation of their standard, which is available online (http://iot.ee.surrey.ac.uk/iot-crawler/ontology/iot-stream). A reference implementation of the *OCF IoT Management and Control* specification has been developed in the IoTivity project. An open-source implementation of OPC UA in the programming language C is open62541 (https://open62541.org). Implementations of the *oneM2M base* ontology and *SSN* ontology are provided as OWL files. *SenML* examples for the different formats, as well as an XML schema are provided in the Internet draft. The *SensorML* specification document provides several examples, as well as XML schemata. Finally, several *Vorto* information models for devices, such as Philips Hue and Bosch XDK, are provided.

5.2.3.5   Criterion ❺: Geolocation Support

Finally, the fifth criterion defines whether the model can describe the (geo-)location of devices, which enables sophisticated features, such as location-based querying. Especially in the IoT, location is important, for example, when recognizing situations, i.e., events that might require a reaction, which occur in a specific room of a smart home.

Some of the surveyed models do not explicitly provide a concept for the modeling of locations. In this case, we analyze whether the models provide a means to be extended with customized properties in order to enable the definition of the location.

homeML provides the element *DeviceLocation*, which can be used to provide the absolute coordinates (x, y, z) of the device. In *IoT ARM*, a *PhysicalEntity* can contain so-called *Tags*, which can be used to model the location of the physical entity in various formats. The *IoT-Lite* ontology and *SensorML* enable the description of locations. The *SSN* ontology enables the description of locations through the DUL (Dolce-UltraLite) ontology, which provides location concepts. Since *IoT-Stream* builds on SSN/SOSA, it also supports geolocation. In their documentation, they also provide an example of how to model geolocation data using their ontology.

Furthermore, the *oneM2M base* ontology does not explicitly describe locations; however, this can be modeled as a *variable*, denoting a property of a device, e.g., the location. In the *OPC UA Information Model*, the location can be defined using the so-called *axis*. Each axis is defined by coordinates (x, y, z). *SenML* also does not explicitly describe locations, but its format can be extended with custom attributes.

IEEE 1451.2 allows the self-description of transducers with respect to static, technical properties. Therefore, locations are not described in TEDS. The *IoT Management and Control standard* and the *IoT-O* ontology do not provide a means to describe locations. Finally, the Eclipse *Vorto* information model does not explicitly support location descriptions.

To summarize, currently, there are many application domains for IoT environments. For example, Gubbi et al. [54] provided the following classification of IoT environments based on implemented testbeds: smart home, smart retail, smart city, smart agriculture, smart water, and smart transportation. Moreover, many models to describe IoT environments exist (cf. Sect. 5.2.2). Therefore, application developers have the difficult task of choosing a suitable model for their IoT applications since, typically, the IoT environment model used in such applications cannot be easily exchanged afterwards.

In Table 5.2, the comparison results based on the introduced criteria are shown. From the surveyed models, homeML is suitable, for example, to describe a smart home, since homeML was explicitly designed for this domain. On the other side, IEEE 1451.2 and OPC UA are rather to be applied in smart factory scenarios. Finally, many models do not define specific domains and are, therefore, generic enough to be employed in different application domains, such as the models IoT ARM, IoT-Lite, IoT-O, oneM2M base, IoT MC, SenML, SensorML, SSN, and Vorto.

Table 5.2 shows that there are several models that fulfill all five criteria, i.e., IoT-Lite, IoT-Stream, oneM2M base, and SSN. Note that our comparison only gives a suggestion about which models are suitable for a generic use, i.e., can be used in different application domains. If for example, a smart home application should be developed, specific domain models, such as homeML, might be more suitable, since it was designed for this specific domain and provides additional means to describe home-related concepts (e.g., rooms, floors, inhabitants). However, generic models can also be employed since they normally can be extended or adapted if needed to meet the requirements of a smart home application. Furthermore, a combination of compatible models (e.g., ontologies) is normally possible as well.

In our comparison, we excluded the analysis of the encoding efficiency of the investigated models. Generally, IoT environment models are not created and processed by resource-constrained IoT devices, but rather by more powerful systems, such as IoT platforms hosted on, for example, cloud infrastructures or servers. Hence, we omitted this aspect of the models in this article. However, it is important to note that specifically ontology-based environment models are heavyweight and require a certain amount of main memory, depending on the size of the ontology. In contrast, JSON-based environment models are more lightweight and, thus, easier to create and process. This enables the handling of such environment models by resource-constrained devices as well. Hence, if it is necessary to process the models on resource-constrained devices or transfer them through resource constrained networks, we recommend using lightweight formats, such as SenML, which is able to create compact descriptions of devices that can be used for discovery purposes.

5.2.4 Other Surveys

Expanding our work, other surveys have also been conducted on the issue of modeling IoT environments.

Compton et al. [55] provided a survey of sensor ontologies. In their work, they focused on the semantic specification of sensors. Their comparison included ontologies such as SWAMO, CSIRO, OntoSensor, and scientific contributions, such as the work introduced by Avancha et al. [56], Matheus et al. [57], or Eid et al. [58]. The criteria for comparison are comprised of (i) sensor specific characteristics, such as sensor hierarchy, identity, manufacturing, contacting, and software, (ii) physical characteristics, such as location, power supply, and operating conditions, (iii) observation specific characteristics, such as accuracy, frequency, and the response model, and (iv) domain specific characteristics, such as units of measurements, feature/quality, or time.

In contrast to Compton et al., our work does not focus on ontologies for the semantic specification of sensors. We compare all kinds of IoT environment models, including semantic and non-semantic models. Furthermore, we do not focus on sensors specifically, but on IoT environments including devices, sensors, and actuators. Moreover, we focus on other criteria, which, in our opinion, are essential to model and describe IoT environments. Finally, most of the models compared by Compton et al. are approximately 10 years old, and newer approaches are therefore missing.

Gyrard et al. [59] created a collection of different vocabularies for the IoT focusing on scientific publications. By doing so, exclusively, ontologies were added to the collection. In contrast, our work focuses not only on ontologies, but on different kinds of models for the IoT.

Chen et al. [60] surveyed several sensor standards, including ECHONET, SensorML, IEEE 1451, Device Kit, and DDL. The authors categorized these standards according to their affiliation to the physical world or the digital world, meaning whether these models describe physical characteristics such as pins or ports or digital characteristics such networking protocols or configuration. In addition, the models were compared regarding the criteria encoding, design perspective, device model, measurement modeling, etc. In our work, we consider non-standard models to enable a wider comparison of the state-of-the-art concepts. Furthermore, this paper was published in the year 2008 and does not consider recent advances in the field of the Internet of Things, including newly emerged models, such as IoT-Lite or the oneM2M base ontology.

Darmois et al. [61] provided a state-of-the-art analysis for IoT standards. Their work was published in the year 2012. Darmois et al. looked at IoT standards in general, not focusing on IoT environment models. They categorized these standards into three layers: (i) the application layer containing high-level IoT applications, (ii) the IoT layer, i.e., the digital representation of the physical world, and (iii) the network layer dealing with the communication. Their overall goal is the recognition of the gaps in the standards of these layers. However, they did not provide a comparison of these standards based on a set of criteria. In contrast, they described existing standards extensively and tried to find gaps that were not addressed by them. Our work does not focus on finding gaps; it aims at providing an overview of existing models to describe IoT environments.

Grangel-González et al. [62] presented a landscape of standards for the Industry 4.0 from a semantic integration perspective. In their work from 2017, they extensively investigated existing standards related to Industry 4.0. These standards include, for example, AML or OPC UA. However, in their work, they did not focus on IoT environment models, but gave an overview of general standards that could be applicable to Industry 4.0. In contrast to their work, the focus of our work does not lie on Industry 4.0, exclusively. We provide an overview of generic existing IoT environment models, applicable to a wide range of scenarios. In addition, we focus on the digital description of these IoT environments and not, for example, on communication standards.

5.2.5   Summary

In this chapter, we present a comparative survey of models that can be employed to describe IoT environments, including devices, their attached sensors, and actuators. Some of the evaluated models have been developed and maintained by large organizations; others have been created in research projects or have been standardized. This survey supports IoT application developers in finding a suitable model for their use cases, as well as researchers in getting an overview of the state-of-the-art IoT environment models.

In order to compare these different models, we define five criteria that summarize important characteristics of the models to be employed in the IoT domain, such as maturity and available implementations. Based on these criteria, we evaluate and compare the surveyed models.

We are aware that many other models exist that could be relevant for our survey, for example the underlying models used by established IoT products in the smart home domain, such as Amazon Echo, Google Home, or ZigBee Alliance Dotdot [63]. However, to keep the focus clear, we considered some exclusion criteria, as described in Sect. 5.2.2. We did not include the IoT standard Dotdot [63], which is a universal application language provided by the ZigBee Alliance for IoT devices, since it focuses mostly on the device-to-device communication and does not provide a holistic description of IoT environments, including all the involved devices, sensors, and actuators. Furthermore, Amazon Echo and Google Home are also not included, since they do not explicitly provide models to describe them as IoT devices and the corresponding IoT environment of which they are a part.

5.3 Setting Up the IoT Environment

After selecting the physical hardware components and creating the IoT Environment Model, the final step of setting up the IoT hardware then deals with the installation process of the hardware. Frigo et al. [1] introduce a business process modeling [64] based approach to guide domain experts and involved stakeholders through the process of setting up their IoT hardware environment. The business process creation is usually conducted by experts. Each process is split into tasks, whereas each task includes setting up one of the previously selected BBIs.

An example of such a process is provided in Fig. 5.18 in BPMN syntax. In this scenario, the goal is setting up a simple IoT hardware environment by connecting a temperature sensor to a Raspberry Pi and connecting it via WiFi to the Microsoft Azure IoT Hub, an IoT platform that allows visualization of IoT data in diagrams. In this example, the domain expert selected the building block implementations: (i) Raspberry Pi, (ii) Temperature sensor KY-028, (iii) WiFi Router, (iv) WiFi connection, and (v) Microsoft Azure IoT Hub.

In order to set up these BBIs, different steps are required that are depicted in the process. Note that setting up a BBI might require a single task in the process, however, others also may require multiple tasks, if setting up the BBI is more complex. This decision is up to the creator of the processes. For manual creation, the BBIs help in selecting the tasks for the creator. Which tasks can be conducted in parallel needs to be decided by the creator as well, hence, some domain knowledge is required for process creation. In doubt, the steps should be conducted sequentially.

After modeling, the process can then be executed in order to realize the setup of the IoT hardware environment. Depending on the chosen BPM language, a

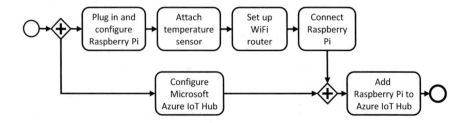

Fig. 5.18 Exemplary BPMN process to set up an IoT application (from Frigo et al. [1])

suitable Business Process Management System (BPMS) needs to be provided. For BPMN 2.0, for example, the established BPMS Camunda[4] could be used. In each step of the process, domain experts get a notification about the tasks they need to conduct, for example, plugging in sensors, configuring a WiFi connection, or installing software on IoT devices. After task completion, the process moves to the next task. Parallelism is usually supported by such BPMS as well.

Once the process has successfully reached its end, the IoT hardware environment is set up. This process can then be reused in similar scenarios, sometimes only with minor necessary adaptations. In case of issues in the processes creation or execution, e.g., due to unforeseen errors, experts need to be available to cope with occurring difficulties and to fix the problems. All occurred problems should then be documented inside the BBI's description so that this knowledge is preserved.

However, it is not unusual that adaptations are necessary over time after an IoT hardware environment was set up. For instance, due to changes in the environment and, hence, changes in the requirements, or due to failing devices that need to be replaced.

If adaptations are necessary, a redefinition of the requirements of the application could be necessary, or adding or removing requirements. The process creation step then creates a so-called *adaptation plan*, which includes removing unnecessary BBIs and only setting up and integrating the newly added ones. After execution of the adaptation plan, the IoT application is set up again, considering the new requirements as well.

Once an IoT application reaches its lifetime, the IoT environment needs to be retired. In this case, the creation of a *termination process* is required, reversing the steps of the original process setting up the application. Using the creation process as a template can ease creation of the termination process. After this process was executed, the IoT hardware environment is retired. We will discuss this further in the final step of our lifecycle method (Sect. 5.10). Note that the creation and termination processes should be stored since they can be useful to re-setup IoT applications after some time.

---

[4] https://camunda.com.

5.4   Modeling the Communication in the IoT Environment

After we modeled the IoT hardware of our environment, it is important to express how these components communicate and, more importantly, which data they share. In this chapter, we describe the *Topic Description Language for the Internet of Things (TDLIoT)*, which we introduced in our previous work [65]. We use an abstraction through *topics* that serve as an endpoint to access device's data or to control them. Each topic usually corresponds to a device, however, depending on the use case, the topic could also correspond to a device's sensor or actuator, leading to potentially multiple topics for a single device.

The TDLIoT provides a simple means to describe and find topics of devices and their sensors and actuators by (i) a holistic description of the topics, (ii) a topic catalog to browse the topic descriptions, and (iii) an effective way to find suitable topics that offer access to the devices' sensors and actuators. In this way, IoT application development can be eased through an abstraction from specific IoT middlewares. The topics can be found, for example, based on a specific location, sensor or actuator type, data types, or data units. We derive requirements for the TDLIoT through expert interviews as well as a scenario in the smart city domain. These requirements form the basis for our prototypical implementation.

We use the Smart Parking scenario, introduced in Chap. 3.2, as basis for deriving requirements and explaining the TDLIoT.

5.4.1   TDLIoT Requirements

In our smart parking scenario, introduced in Chap. 3.2, we assume that different parking space providers offer different parking spaces throughout a larger city. By doing so, they use different means to provide information about their parking spots (e.g., occupation) and for booking them. In order to build an application that gives an overview of all parking spaces and to conduct bookings through it, it is necessary to define how the information of these different providers can be accessed.

Since these providers use different protocols and interfaces, we need a means to define how the IoT data can be accessed. This means should be provided by the TDLIoT, a uniform format to specify which data can be accessed by IoT devices and how they can be controlled by IoT applications.

For our scenario, we aim for an open catalog providing all available TDLIoT definitions for the different parking spots of the city. By accessing the catalog, IoT application developers can get an overview which parking spaces exist and can implement their application according to the provided APIs and protocols of their providers. In our previous work [65], we defined the following requirements for our TDLIoT definition:

(*A*) **Genericness**   As mentioned before and emphasized in our use case scenario, IoT environments are very heterogeneous with respect to the existence of different devices, sensors, and actuators. In order to develop a future-proof topic description, the TDLIoT is required to be generic in a way that it supports all kinds of devices, sensors, and actuators, and is not restricted to a specific kind of hardware. Furthermore, different protocols and message formats are being created regularly for the IoT and the TDLIoT should be able to support these as well.

(B) **Technology independency**   In a similar manner, the technologies used in the IoT are very heterogeneous. Many communication protocols, gateways, and middleware solutions exist to build IoT applications. Therefore, the TDLIoT concepts need to be technology-independent in order to be realized, for example, using different protocols.

(C) **Self-containment**   A TDLIoT description needs to be self-contained, which means it contains all required information to describe, find, and access topics of sensors and actuators. Consequently, it should not be necessary to access external sources to retrieve additional information about the topics of interest.

(D) **Lightweightness**   The TDLIoT needs to be lightweight in order to support IoT scenarios with limited resources. More precisely, the size of TDLIoT descriptions should be compact, which requires choosing lightweight data formats, such as JSON or YAML. Furthermore, the TDLIoT should be kept as simple as possible to reduce the required effort to get familiar with it.

(E) **Extensibility**   Similar to the need for genericness, the TDLIoT should be extensible with new attributes in the future due to the constantly changing IoT resources. Hence, high extensibility is of vital importance.

5.4.2   Topic Description Language for the IoT

In this section, we introduce the Topic Description Language for the IoT and how it can be employed by IoT applications. Our approach is depicted in Fig. 5.19. It is composed of three main roles: the *topic provider*, the *topic consumer*, and the *topic catalog*. The topic provider creates *topic descriptions* based on the TDLIoT and publishes them to the topic catalog. The topic consumer searches for interesting topic descriptions in the topic catalog, and directly connects to topic providers to either publish data or receive the data published to subscribed topics. These roles are described in detail in Sects. 5.4.2.2–5.4.2.4.

This approach is inspired by the Service Oriented Architecture (SOA) Triangle [72], which provides a means to discover and bind services. In Sect. 5.4.3, we explain how we differ from the traditional SOA approach. In the following sections, we explain in detail (i) how to describe topics using the TDLIoT, and (ii) how to publish and retrieve topics from the topic catalog.

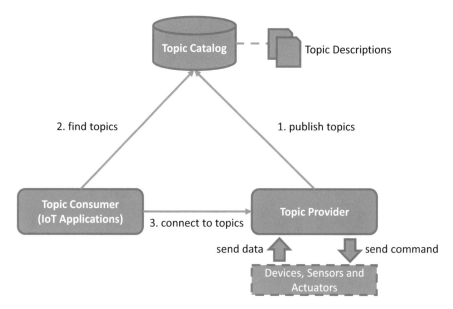

Fig. 5.19 Overview of the approach for topic description and retrieval (based on Franco da Silva et al. [65])

5.4.2.1   Topic Description

In this section, we describe the content and structure of a *topic description* using the TDLIoT. Each topic description contains several attributes. Their values are represented as strings. We use examples from the motivating scenario described in Sect. 3.2 to clarify the TDLIoT attributes:

- **data type** the data type of the values provided by the topic, e.g., *boolean*, which is *true* if the parking space is occupied or *false* otherwise
- **hardware type** *(optional)* the type of hardware represented by the topic, i.e., a specific sensor or actuator, e.g., *occupation detection sensor*
- **location** the location of the sensor or actuator represented by the topics. It contains the *location type*, e.g., GPS or a specific city name, as well as the *location value*, e.g., specific *GPS coordinates*
- **message format** the format of the message provided by the topic, e.g., *JSON*, *YAML*, or *XML*
- **message structure** the structure of the message defined as metamodel to understand its content. It contains the *metamodel type*, e.g., *JSON schema* or *XML schema* and the specific *metamodel*
- **middleware endpoint** the endpoint of the IoT middleware hosting the topic, e.g., the endpoint of a message broker running on a server
- **owner** the name of the topic provider, e.g., *City of Stuttgart*
- **path** path of the topic, e.g., */parking-space-monitor*

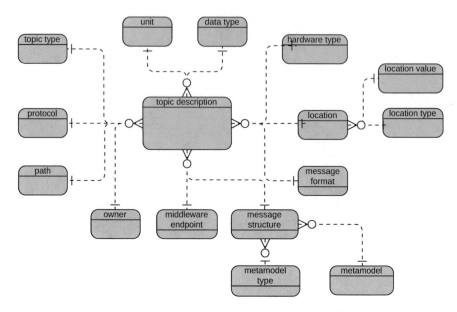

Fig. 5.20 Data model associated with the TDLIoT (based on Franco da Silva et al. [65])

- **protocol** the communication protocol being used, e.g., *MQTT* or *HTTP*
- **topic type** the type of the topic, i.e., *subscription* or *command*
- **unit** *(optional)* the unit of the data provided through the topic, e.g., *Celsius* if the topic provides temperature values in degree Celsius

Figure 5.20 shows the TDLIoT metamodel as entity-relation model in the notation of Chen [66]. This model describes the relations between the entities of TDLIoT descriptions. Apart from the *hardware type* and *unit* attributes, all of its entities must only occur once within a single TDLIoT description. However, these entities could occur in an arbitrary amount of descriptions, hence, they are not globally unique. In case topics provide aggregated data, originating from different sensors, or data that does not originate from hardware at all, the *hardware type* attribute is not required.

A special case for the TDLIoT is a sensor that measures different values at once and sends them within a single message, i.e., a multisensor. An example is the sensor ZigBee ZBS-121,[5] which measures temperature, brightness, and detects motion. Consequently, the attributes *data type* and *unit* would have to occur multiple times, i.e., for each measured value of the multisensor. In order to avoid matching issues, the data type attribute should, for example, have the value *MultiSensorDataType*. Note that the *data type* attribute can be useful in the TDLIoT, even though this information is redundant in the *message structure* attribute. When searching for

---

[5] ZigBee ZBS-121: http://www.pikkerton.de/_objects/1/26.htm.

suitable topic descriptions, the data type of the (e.g., sensor) values could be an important criteria. This attribute directly provides the underlying data type and omits a message parsing overhead. Furthermore, the *topic type* attribute indicates whether this topic can be subscribed to or whether it is used to publish command messages, e.g., to actuators.

To prevent conflicts or confusion regarding the values of the TDLIoT attributes, ontologies can be used to detail the semantic description of these values, such as a specific hardware type having more than one name. For example, the type *occupation detection sensor* could also be named *parking sensor* or *PSensor* in different topic descriptions. Grangel-Gonzalez et al. [67] introduce such a ontology-based vocabulary for the IoT based on ontologies, which can be used as foundation for this work. Furthermore, other semantic relations can be expressed through the ontology, for example, whether the represented hardware is a sensor or actuator. Using such a vocabulary enhances the TDL with semantics, i.e., the meaning of attribute values can be understood through reasoning approaches. Without this semantic information, finding topic descriptions for specific use cases can become difficult.

When creating topic descriptions, topic providers can query such an ontology in order to find out the specific attribute values they can use, e.g., the type name of the hardware represented by the topic. Only names appearing in the ontology vocabulary should be used in the topic descriptions. New names, for example, of a new type of sensor, should be added to the vocabulary first. The goal of Grangel-Gonzalez et al. [67] is to accomplish a common vocabulary for the IoT, which all involved partners (e.g., sensor manufacturers) agree on. In their case, they specifically focus on the domain Industrie 4.0. However, such a vocabulary could be provided for a wide range of domains. We do not focus on the specific characteristics of such ontologies since it has already been intensively discussed by Grangel-Gonzalez et al [67].

As an example for the TDLIoT, we show a topic description for the motivating scenario based on the JavaScript Object Notation (JSON) in Listing 5.1. We choose this format because it is lightweight and established in the IoT domain. In this example, a topic description based on the TDLIoT is shown for an occupation detection sensor. This description contains all the information necessary to connect and subscribe to the represented topic. Through the *endpoint* attribute value, the topic can be reached using the defined protocol, in this case MQTT. This information is sufficient to subscribe to this topic and receive messages. To develop IoT applications that can automatically process these messages, the *message structure* is described inside the topic description using JSON schema. This metamodel contains information about the data structure and the data types. The JSON schema can be used to derive or implement parsers for the messages received from the topic. The other attributes of the description, such as location, path, hardware type, or owner, can be used to search for the topic description in the topic catalog. For example, an IoT application developer aiming to implement the smart parking application of our scenario might search for all topics representing sensors of type *occupation detection sensor* in *Stuttgart*.

```
{ "data_type": "boolean",
  "hardware_type": "occupation detection sensor",
  "location": {
      "location_type": "city name",
      "location_value": "Stuttgart"
  },
  "message_format": "JSON",
  "message_structure": {
    "metamodel_type": "JSON schema",
    "metamodel":"{"title": "provider_schema",
                  "type": "object",
                  "properties": {
                     "value": {"type": "boolean"},
                     "timestamp": {"type": "integer"},
                     "time_up": {"type": "string"} },
                  "required": ["value", "timestamp"]}"
  },
  "middleware_endpoint": "http://example.com",
  "owner": "city-of-stuttgart",
  "path": "/parking-space-monitor",
  "protocol": "MQTT",
  "topic_type": "subscription"
}
```

Listing 5.1 Example of a topic description based on JSON (based on Franco da Silva et al. [65])

5.4.2.2   Topic Provider

In our approach, the topic provider can be any entity that owns hardware that either produces data (e.g., sensors) or that allows to perform certain activities (e.g., actuators), and wants to make this hardware available to further applications. In our motivating scenario, a topic provider is a parking area owner that deployed several sensors in parking spaces to monitor the current occupancy state. Providing access to these sensor data allows application developers to create applications to, for example, dynamically detect unoccupied parking spaces.

The topic provider usually provides an IoT middleware, which hosts and manages topics for sensors and actuators. This is depicted in Fig. 5.19 at the bottom right. Furthermore, the topic provider knows specific information about their sensors and actuators (e.g., hardware type) and how to access them (e.g., endpoint, protocol). In order to enable sensors and actuators to be discovered as topics, the topic provider creates topic descriptions for them using the TDLIoT. An example of a topic description for an occupancy detection sensor can be seen in Listing 5.1. This description contains all information necessary to find topics and bind to a selected topic.

The topic descriptions can be published to the topic catalog and are retrievable by topic consumers. Furthermore, once a topic is published, the topic providers can either update a topic description, e.g., when the endpoint to the IoT middleware changes, or delete a topic, for example, when the topic owner does not want to allow access to its hardware anymore.

5.4.2.3 Topic Consumer

In our approach, the topic consumer can be any entity that wants to receive sensor data or send commands to actuators. For example, sensor data could be used to build IoT applications, such as a monitoring dashboard [68]. In our motivating scenario, a topic consumer is an application developer aiming to develop a GPS-based smart phone application to detect unoccupied parking spaces near to the current location of the drivers.

To do so, the developer requires access to sensors detecting parking space occupancy, and actuators that can be controlled, for example, gates that enable access to parking spaces and that can be automatically opened. Imaging multiple parking spot providers that have different sensors and actuators deployed and require different access protocols. Topic consumers need to find the most suitable topics for their applications, which could depend on the location of the parking spot, the data types of the sensor values, or the protocol used. In order to develop such applications, the topic consumer searches for interesting topic descriptions in the topic catalog, for example, for topic descriptions of *occupancy detection sensors* at the location *Stuttgart*. An example for such a search can be seen in Listing 5.4. Once topic consumers find relevant topic descriptions, they can directly bind to the corresponding topics. The necessary binding information, i.e., the endpoint, the topic names, the required message structure, and protocol, is contained in the topic description.

It is also possible that two different topics exist that represent the same sensor or actuator. For example, one topic could provide the sensor data in the JSON format, the other one in an XML representation. The topic consumer can then choose the most fitting topic description to build the desired application. Furthermore, based on the topic descriptions, topic consumers could automatically generate code stubs for the binding to the corresponding topics through parsing the message structure from the corresponding catalog entry.

5.4.2.4 Topic Catalog and REST API

The topic catalog contains a data store for topics described in TDLIoT notation. It provides a REST API to enable topic providers to publish topic descriptions and topic consumers to retrieve those descriptions. To publish a topic to the topic catalog, topic providers first need to model their topics in the description structure presented in Sect. 5.4.2.1 and exemplified in Listing 5.1 and then submit these descriptions to the topic catalog through its REST API.

```
POST /topics HTTP/1.1
Content-Type: application/json

{ "data_type": "boolean",
  "hardware_type": "occupation detection sensor", ... }

HTTP/1.1 201 CREATED
topic_id: 7321
```

Listing 5.2 Example of publishing a new topic to the catalog based on JSON (based on Franco da Silva et al. [65])

```
GET /topics HTTP/1.1
Accept: application/json

HTTP/1.1 200 OK
[ {"data_type": "boolean", ...},
  {"data_type": "float", ...}, ... ]
```

Listing 5.3 Requesting all registered topics from the catalog (based on Franco da Silva et al. [65])

An example of how to use the API to submit a new topic to the catalog is shown in Listing 5.2. In this example, the topic depicted in Listing 5.1 should be added to the topic catalog. To do so, a HTTP POST request is sent to the topic catalog, in this example, being available through the resource URI */topics*. The header of this request contains the data format of the TDLIoT description, in this case JSON. In the body, the TDLIoT description itself is provided. The response of the request contains a unique id for the created topic, *topic_id*, which is generated by the topic catalog. With the topic id, topic providers can either change a topic description or remove it.

However, changes in the topic descriptions could lead to issues by topic consumers that are currently using the topics, for example, when the endpoint or message structure changes. This also concerns deletion of topic descriptions. To cope with these issues, the topic catalog provides a means to register on changes in the topic descriptions. For that, the topic consumer needs to provide a callback endpoint to which notifications about changes are send to. When using NoSQL databases to store topic descriptions, such notification functionality is usually provided natively, for example, in CouchDB [69]. However, this requires versioning of the topic descriptions. This is not yet considered in our approach, however, it can be achieved by adding an additional version attribute to the TDLIoT.

The topic catalog allows topic consumers to search for interesting topics through the provided API. For that, topic consumers either request a list of all published topics and browse this list manually or conduct a refined search by specifying filters for the topics. Listing 5.3 shows how to use the API to list all registered topics in the catalog. To realize this, a HTTP GET request is sent to the topic catalog URI. The type of the description can be defined by the *Accept* header attribute of the HTTP request. This is especially important if TDLIoT descriptions exist in several data formats (e.g., JSON, XML, etc.). If no accept header is specified, the JSON representation is returned by the catalog.

```
POST /topics HTTP/1.1
Accept: application/json  Content-Type: application/json

{ "filters": {
    "location": {
        "location_type": "city name",
        "location_value": "Stuttgart"
    },
    "hardware_type": "occupation detection sensor"
  } }

HTTP/1.1  200  OK
[ {"data_type": "boolean", ...},
  {"data_type": "float", ...}, ... ]
```

Listing 5.4 Requesting occupation detection topics located in Stuttgart (based on Franco da Silva et al. [65])

To realize a refined search, topic consumers specify filters based on the attributes defined in Sect. 5.4.2.1. For example, if a topic consumer is interested in all registered *occupation detection* topics located in *Stuttgart*, a refined search by hardware type and location can be used, as shown in Listing 5.4. Based on the specified filter, the topic catalog generates queries that are executed by the data store of TDLIoT descriptions. Finally, the found descriptions are returned to the topic consumers. When querying the TDLIoT descriptions based on its attributes, the catalog can check the aforementioned ontology (cf. Sect. 5.4.2.1) for synonyms of the values in order to query for all suitable topics, even though their attributes are named differently. In this way, topic consumers can also retrieve related topics that fulfill their requirements.

When providing the topic catalog in a centralized manner, this could lead to scalability issues and become a single point of failure. Consequently, a distributed, replicated data store, such as CouchDB, should be used in combination with cloud computing capabilities. In this way, the topic catalog can be scaled throughout a large number of instances (even automatically) and, thus, scalability issues can be reduced significantly.

Similar to web services, after finding suitable topics in the topic catalog, topic consumers still need to negotiate the specific usage terms with the topic providers. For example, access control mechanisms could be in place, which requires a generation of access tokens in order to connect to the topics. Such tokens need to be exchanged directly between topic providers and consumers. Consequently, access control and other specific usage terms need to be handled by the topic consumers and providers themselves. This is not in the scope of the topic catalog.

5.4.2.5 Prototypical Implementation

We implemented an open-source prototype available on github under the Apache 2.0 license[6] The prototype is also available in Docker hub[7] The topic catalog was implemented using MongoDB[8] to store and manage the topic descriptions, which are in JSON notation. Moreover, we created the proposed REST API to access the topic catalog. The used REST framework is Java Spring.[9] A documentation of the API is provided using Swagger.[10] We provide a Java-based client application to access the topic catalog and subscribe to and publish to topics using the MQTT protocol. Finally, we provide a web user interface, in which the current topic descriptions are visualized and can be edited through the REST API.

5.4.3 Related Work

Grangel-González et al. [67] introduce a vocabulary for the Internet of Things, especially for the domains Industrie 4.0 and smart cities. This vocabulary is based on ontologies, thus, defining semantic relations between entities in the IoT, e.g., devices, sensors, and actuators. In our approach, we use this vocabulary as basis for the attribute values that can be used in the TDLIoT descriptions. By doing so, we can avoid confusion or conflicts when creating such descriptions.

A common API for publish-subscribe was proposed by Pietzuch et al. [70], which supports three levels of compliance: (i) the lowest level, specifying abstract operations, (ii) the middle level, describing interactions using a light-weighted XML-RPC mechanism, and (iii) the highest level, enforcing a XML-RPC data model. In our approach, we provide an API as well, however, we aim at facilitating the description and querying of topics. The specific realization of the communication between topic providers and topic consumers is out of scope.

Dai et al. [71] argue that WSDL does not enable the description of an IoT object with all its information, since WSDL does not provide methods to represent non-functional aspects of services. Therefore, they propose a flexible extension of WSDL to describe non-functional attributes, so that it enables the complete description of a physical IoT object, including what it is and what it can do. In our approach, we aim at the description of an IoT object in the form of topics. In addition, we provide means to search for interesting topics based on IoT object attribute values, such as unit (e.g., Celsius) or location (e.g., Stuttgart).

---

[6] Github repository: https://github.com/IPVS-AS/TDLIoT.

[7] Dockerhub repository: https://hub.docker.com/r/ipvs/tdl-catalogue/.

[8] MongoDB: https://www.mongodb.com/.

[9] Java Spring: https://spring.io/.

[10] Swagger: https://swagger.io/.

In service-oriented architectures (SOA) [72, 73], similar roles exist to enable building applications based on services. The roles Service Provider, Service Consumer, and Universal Description, Discovery and Integration (UDDI), also referred as *SOA Triangle*, match the described roles topic provider, topic consumer, and topic catalog. The SOA Triangle is an approved means to find services, therefore, we build on these concepts and apply them to topics in the IoT. In the UDDI, different so-called *pages* exist. In the *white* pages, information about the service provider are stored, including how they can be contacted. In the *yellow* pages, services are being classified based on their attributes. This is necessary to find them effectively. Finally, in the *green* pages, the concrete interface specification of the services are contained, i.e., how to access them. In contrast to the UDDI, our approach does not differentiate among these pages. All information contained in these pages is integrated within a single TDLIoT description. Due to the fact that this information is very lightweight, it does not need to be split up onto several pages. The overview can still be kept clear.

The Web Service Description Language (WSDL) [74] is an approved means to describe web services [72]. When using messaging, there is usually a SOAP/JMS binding available [75]. In our approach, we aim for a lightweight, easy to use way to describe topics. The TDLIoT is tailored for topics in the IoT and uses terms specific to it. Realizing these concepts using WSDL is possible, as shown by Dai et al. [71]. However, an approach specialized to the needs of the IoT (see Sect. 5.4.1) could lead to simplified and more intuitive application development.

Jimenez et al. [76] introduce IPSO Smart Objects, an abstraction of communication protocols, such as HTTP or the Constrained Application Protocol (CoAP) [77]. The goal is to provide high level interoperability between devices and connected software applications. Furthermore, the Open Mobile Alliance Lightweight Specification (OMA LWM2M) [78] is used, which provides a set of management interfaces based on CoAP.

However, even though the IPSO Smart Objects provide a good abstraction to access devices in the IoT, there are no means to browse available devices and to find the most suitable one to develop a specific IoT application. Combining the TDLIoT with resource description standards, such as IPSO, OMA LWM2M, or early approaches, such as UPnP, is currently not considered in our first approach but will be part of our future work.

In summary, we enabled a SOA-inspired approach to describe topics in the IoT. Current approaches extend WSDL in order to achieve this goal. However, in our approach, we aim for a low complexity and a very lightweight description of topics tailor-made for the IoT. This can be achieved through the TDLIoT.

5.4.4 Summary

For communication in the IoT environment, we described the Topic Description Language for the Internet of Things (TDLIoT), which enables a simple means to describe and find topics of sensors and actuators by providing (i) a description of the topics, (ii) a catalog to browse the topic descriptions, and (iii) an effective way to query and find suitable topics. In this way, IoT application development can be eased through an appropriate abstraction from specific IoT middlewares. The topics can be found, for example, based on a specific location, sensor or actuator type. The TDLIoT descriptions build on a data model that defines their content.

Our approach defines three roles. The topic provider, which creates topic descriptions representing their sensor and actuator and publishes them to the topic catalog. The topic catalog, storing the topic descriptions, and enabling effective means to query them. Finally, the topic consumer, searching for suitable topics to build IoT applications. How the topic catalog can be queried is simplified by a REST-based API, which abstracts from the specific query languages.

To show the applicability of our approach, we present a motivating scenario in the domain smart cities, which describes a smart parking application based on topic descriptions. In this application, occupation sensors and actuators to open gates to the parking spaces are represented by corresponding topics described using the TDLIoT. Furthermore, we provide an open-source prototype of our concepts that is available online.[11]

In future work, we plan to describe non-functional properties of the topics, such as availability, costs, or quality of service, e.g., the accuracy of a provided sensor value. This can be achieved by extending the TDLIoT with new attributes.

Furthermore, we plan to integrate service level agreements (SLA) [79] so that topic providers and consumers can agree on specific usage conditions. Moreover, through the integration of the introduced topic descriptions into access control frameworks [80], security mechanisms can be provided.

5.5   IoT Software Design and Implementation

After the physical hardware environment has been planned and set up, and the available topics have been modeled using the TDLIoT, the next step comprises the design and implementation of the software components considering the capabilities of the installed hardware and the available topics.

Since devices in the IoT are very heterogeneous, developing corresponding IoT software applications can be very cumbersome [81]. For example, there are powerful devices, such as Raspberry Pis,[12] able to provide an operating system and built-in communication technologies, such as WiFi or Bluetooth. In contrast, there are very restricted devices, such as micro-controller boards, that do not provide any sophisticated operating system but rather a limited runtime environment to run small scripts, usually implemented in the C programming language. Some of these

---

[11] https://github.com/IPVS-AS/TDLIoT.

[12] https://www.raspberrypi.org/,

restricted devices provide a WiFi connection, others require Bluetooth or need to be connected via cable. Hence, software needs to be tailored to the specific IoT devices.

Furthermore, in the IoT, not only the devices are very heterogeneous but also the communication channels and protocols to be used, e.g., CoAP [77], MQTT [82], or HTTP. This makes software development for IoT applications even more complex. Consequently, there is a demand for coping with this large heterogeneity and to support IoT application developers in making the right choices when it comes to developing their software for the available hardware and network technology.

To cope with this issue, the process of selecting suitable software components can also be done using the introduced IoT toolbox, which is based on the work of Frigo et al. [1]. By doing so, the hardware BBs and BBIs need to be extended by software-specific BBIs, which can be, once again, recommended based on a set of requirements.

Furthermore, similar to the hardware setup, we can use a business process based approach to set up the IoT applications based on the suggested building blocks.

Analog to the hardware BBI selection process, in a first step, domain experts and involved stakeholders discuss the requirements of their IoT application according to existing hardware components and create a specification document for it. These requirements include, for example, efficiency, security, or robustness. After that, in the second step, domain experts find suitable software building blocks based on the requirements in the toolbox. Then, a business process is created based on the selected building blocks, defining the necessary steps that need to be undertaken to set them up. Next, this process is executed, guiding the domain experts in the process of setting up their application. Finally, the IoT application is tested and, if there are no changes necessary, it goes into production. The IoT application is retired once it reaches its lifetime.

5.5.1 Software Building Blocks

We introduced the structure of the building blocks in Sect. 5.1. Here, we extend the toolbox with software-specific BBs and BBIs. On the right of Fig. 5.21, an example building block is given for the communication paradigm publish-subscribe, enabling loosely coupled communication. As mentioned before, each BB has one or more implementations attached to it, which are referred to as building block implementation (BBI). These BBIs are concrete implementations of a BB. In case of software components, a BBI contains a software artifact, which can be of different types, e.g., a Docker container, a cloud service, or a binary application. Furthermore, BBIs can have a set of dependencies that could require installation of different BBIs. For example, some BBIs might require the installation of certain programming languages (Java, Python) or a specific operating system. In addition, each BBI requires a definition of its interfaces to enable an easy orchestration via business processes. In case of service based software artifacts, these interface descriptions should be defined based on standards, such as WSDL [72].

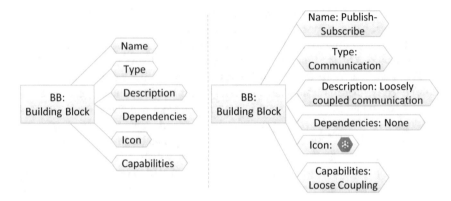

Fig. 5.21 Left: Remainder of a building block; Right: Building block example for publish-subscribe communication

For our BB example in Fig. 5.21, implementations include MQTT brokers, such as Mosquitto[13] or RabbitMQ.[14] Once domain experts decide to use the publish-subscribe paradigm, they will find the according building block in the toolbox and will be able to select one of the corresponding implementations.

Figure 5.22 depicts an example of hierarchical software building blocks using the message broker example. In this example, as a root, a very generic building block "Communication Module" is defined, representing all possible kinds of communication components. This BB is then derived to the "Message Broker" building block, which represent all message brokers that are able to enable communication, or to other communication means. The Message Broker BB can then be derived again, for example, to MQTT based brokers represented by a corresponding BB. This BB then has two different implementations, which can again be derived by other BBIs. In this example, HiveMQ can be provided in the Commercial or Community version.

Once again, after the IoT Toolbox is filled with BBs and BBIs, in a first step, IoT application developers, i.e., the domain experts, and their stakeholders need to define a set of requirements for their application. These requirements need to consider different aspects, such as network capabilities, used communication paradigms, costs, efficiency, security, privacy, available computer resources, and so on. Defining such requirements requires involving many different stakeholders and technical experts for each of these areas.

Based on the resulting set of requirements, BBs and BBIs can be selected. The matching needs to be done by the domain experts themselves by browsing the toolbox and finding the building blocks with suitable capabilities. Even though the matching step currently needs to be done manually, the toolbox gives a

---

[13] Mosquitto Message Broker: https://mosquitto.org/.

[14] RabbitMQ Message Broker: https://www.rabbitmq.com/.

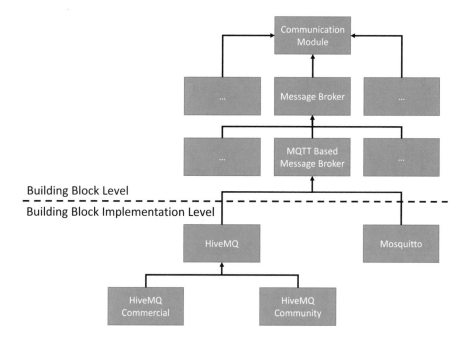

Fig. 5.22 Hierarchy of building blocks, example for a message broker

good overview regarding which technologies and approaches are available for IoT applications without the need for domain experts to acquire this knowledge themselves.

In a second step, domain experts and involved stakeholders browse the toolbox and select the building blocks they need to fulfill their requirements.

After that, using business processes [64], domain experts and involved stakeholders can be guided through the process of setting up their IoT application. An example of such a process is provided in Fig. 5.23 in BPMN syntax. In this scenario, the goal is setting up a simple IoT application that sends temperature measurements to a dashboard running in a backend cloud for visualization of the temperature data in diagrams. The previously selected hardware component BBIs were a Raspberry Pi and a modular temperature sensor that was attached to it using the Raspberry Pi's GPIO interface. In this example, the domain expert selects the building block implementations: (i) Mosquitto MQTT for messaging, (ii) Python for the MQTT client implementation on Raspberry Pi and backend cloud, (iii) and the dashboard that can be installed in the backend cloud. In this process, first, the Mosquitto and Python libraries need to be installed on the Raspberry Pi. Next, the MQTT client, publishing the temperature data, needs to be installed and started on the Raspberry Pi and the corresponding subscriber that fetches the data needs to be installed in

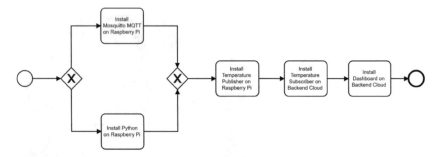

Fig. 5.23 Exemplary BPMN process to set up an IoT application

the backend cloud. Finally, the dashboard application needs to be installed and connected to the MQTT subscriber.

Once the process has successfully reached its end, the IoT application is set up. This process can then be reused in similar scenarios, sometimes only with minor necessary adaptations. In case of issues in the processes creation or execution, e.g., due to unforeseen errors, experts need to be available to cope with occurring difficulties and to fix the problems. All occurred problems should then be documented inside the BBI's description so that this knowledge is preserved. Another approach to set up the IoT application automatically is introduced in Sect. 5.6, using the TOSCA standard.

5.5.2 Data Processing Model

After the BBIs for the software components have been selected and set up, it needs to be defined how they work together and which data they exchange. To do so, in our previous work [84], we introduce a data processing model, defining a pipeline, modeling the data flow of an IoT application.

Interactions between devices in IoT applications can be described by directed graphs according to the pipes-and-filters design pattern [85], which we refer to as the *data processing model* in the following. In our experience, and as shown in related work (e.g., [84, 120]), the pipes and filters pattern is appropriate to describe the behavior of IoT environments.

Nodes in the data processing model, i.e., the filters, are referred to as *operations* and are not bound to specific devices. Instead, they are associated with a set of *requirements*, making it possible to dynamically choose the right device for the operator.

We define the data processing model as a tupel $DF = (O, E, R, req)$ with the set of operations O, the set of directed edges $E = \{e = (o_i, o_j) | o_i, o_j \in O\}$, stating that operation o_i must be performed right before operation o_j, the set of requirements R, and the function $req : O \to \mathcal{P}(R)$, which links each operation to a

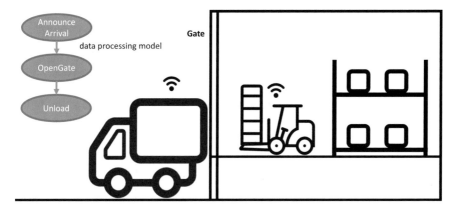

Fig. 5.24 Loading of a truck by an autonomous forklift (based on Del Gaudio et al. [84])

set of requirements. An example for a data processing model of our introduced IoT scenario (Sect. 3.1) in JSON representation looks as follows:

```
{
   "flow_id": "UnloadingFlow",
   "flow": {
     "1": {
       "operation": "AnnounceArrival",
       "requirements": ["PositionSensor"],
       "next_oiid": "2"
     },
     "2": {
       "operation": "OpenGate",
       "requirements": ["GateController"],
       "next_oiid": "3"
     },
     "3": {
       "operation": "Unload",
       "requirements":
         ["Forklift", "PositionSensor"],
       "next_oiid": none
     },
   }
}
```

In this example, `flow_id` defines a unique name for each data processing model. Each sub-element of `flow` represents an operation. `next_oiid` indicates which operation must be executed after `AnnounceArrival` and so forth. The data processing model is depicted in Fig. 5.24. The first operation `AnnounceArrival` is executed by `SmartTruck` by sending its position data to `SmartGate` to announce its arrival. It uses the data to execute `OpenGate` and tell the next available `AutonomousForklift` to unload the Truck.

Using this model, it can be defined how the data should flow through the IoT environment to fulfill the functionality of the IoT application.

5.6   IoT Software Deployment

After selection of the software modules that form the IoT application, an important step is their deployment. Especially in the IoT, deployment can become very cumbersome since software is usually distributed over hundreds or thousands of different devices, offering heterogeneous interfaces, operating systems, or, in the worst case, need to be flashed manually. Hence, there is a desire to automate the deployment process as much as possible.

For the deployment of software, an advanced model based approach is using the standard Topology and Orchestration Specification for Cloud Applications (TOSCA). Even though the word Cloud is in the title, this standard has been extended in other works [86, 87] to fit not only the requirements of virtual cloud environments but also of physical environment, such as the Internet of Things.

5.6.1   TOSCA Foundations

Figure 5.25 shows the structure of a TOSCA Service Template. In TOSCA, a Service Template describes the application to be deployed including all necessary infrastructure, platform, and application components. Hence, the whole stack of an application can be modeled to cover complex deployment scenarios in which not only application components are set up but also infrastructure and platform components.

As depicted, a Service Template contains four important concepts: Topology Templates, Node Types, Relationship Types, and Plans.

The Topology Template is describing dependencies and relationship of the involved components, e.g., that a specific component is *hosted on* another component or that a component *connects* to another component, for example, when an application connects to a database. The nodes of the Topology Template are called Node Templates and they stand for a self-contained software module or service. The edges in a Topology Template are called Relationship Templates and describe how the components are connected.

Node Types define the structure of Node Templates, thus, defining the interfaces, properties, requirements, and capabilities. For each Node Template of the Topology Template, a corresponding Node Type must exist. Relationship Types work analog to Node Types and define, in a similar manner, the structure of Relationship Templates. Node Templates and Relationship Templates can be attached with so-called Implementation Artifacts and Deployment artifacts which are essentially pieces of code, implementing their business logic or binary objects that are required for deployment or operation of the application.

Finally, Plans define the steps and their order that need to be undertaken to set up the application based on the Topology Template. For example, first, the infrastructure components need to be set up before any platform or application

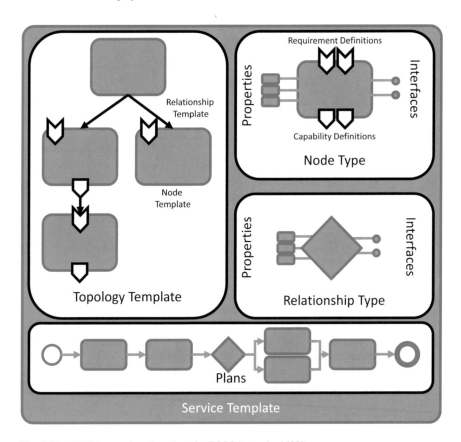

Fig. 5.25 TOSCA overview (based on the TOSCA standard [88])

components need to be installed. This is defined by these Plans. Furthermore, Breitenbuecher et al. [89], introduce an approach to automatically generate this plan based on the Relationship Types indicating the order how the different modules should be set up. In addition to the previously mentioned Relationship Templates *hosted on* and *connects to*, *depends on* can be used to make sure that one component is required to be set up before the other since it depends on it.

Another important concept in TOSCA are Requirements and Capabilities as shown in Fig. 5.26. Requirements, defined by so-called Requirement Definition, and Capabilities, defined by Capability Definitions, offer a means to make sure that Node Templates can be connected to each other, i.e., are compatible. Each Requirement fits with a corresponding Capability in a key-lock fashion. This is an essential concept to ensure that no components are connected that do not fit together. For example, in this manner, it can be avoided that a Python-based application is deployed into a Java application server, such as Apache Tomcat.

Finally, after all Node Types, Relationship Types, Topology Templates, Plans, and so on have been modeled, they are put together into a self-contained package

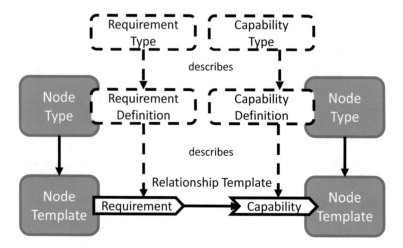

Fig. 5.26 TOSCA requirement and capabilities (based on [88])

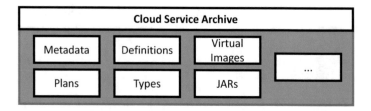

Fig. 5.27 TOSCA cloud service archive (based on [88])

called the TOSCA Cloud Service Archive (CSAR). Hence, a CSAR contains all
components required to set up an application, also including the implementations,
libraries, and so on. However, in practice, larger binary elements are usually
outsourced and only referenced within the CSAR, which violates the self-contained
requirement however, also leads to a very large package to be processed by TOSCA
engines. The structure of a CSAR is shown in Fig. 5.27.

5.6.2 TOSCA and the Internet of Things

The TOSCA standard offers a suitable means to deploy IoT applications throughout
distributed and heterogeneous infrastructures. In the following, we describe the
approach of Franco da Silva et al. [86] to deploy IoT applications using the TOSCA
standard.

As shown in Fig. 5.28, in TOSCA, different stacks can be modeled and connected
through Node and Relationship Templates. We hereby separate three different
stacks, namely (i) the IoT Application Stack, modeling all software components

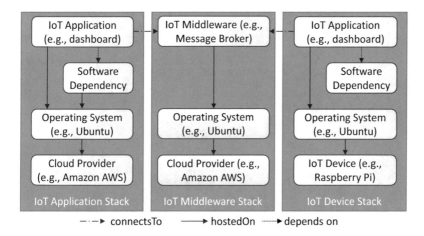

Fig. 5.28 Structure of a TOSCA topology for the IoT (based on Franco da Silva et al. [86])

of the application itself, (ii) the IoT Middleware Stack, comprising different components for necessary communication middleware between the physical hardware and the IoT application, and (iii) the IoT Device Stack, comprising of the software components being deployed directly onto the IoT hardware.

According to our introduced life cycle, the deployment model would be built from the right, starting with all the software to be deployed onto the physical IoT hardware. Next, the middleware stack would be modeled, and finally the IoT Application Stack. Now, if it comes to the deployment of multiple Smart Device Stacks, which is typically the case if there are many IoT devices involved, the Smart Device Stack should be modeled separately so it can be instantiated for each device with different parameterization.

Figure 5.29 shows an example of a TOSCA topology for an IoT application measuring the temperature of a Smart Home. The involved BBIs include a Python implementation to measure the temperature of an attached sensor to a Raspberry Pi, a Mosquitto message broker, using MQTT for communication, and an IoT platform implemented in Python, hosted in a Cloud environment.

After modeling, this TOSCA topology can be instantiated. In this step, parameters need to be given, such as the IP address and credentials of the Raspberry Pi, to be able to deploy the application into it. Using the plan generator by Breitenbücher et al. [89], the TOSCA plan can be generated automatically.

Figure 5.30 shows an exemplary build plan for the IoT application step of Fig. 5.29. As can be seen, the TOSCA plan defines all steps necessary to set up an IoT application's software. Note that these plan could involve manual steps as well and cannot necessarily be fully automated.

Once implementation of TOSCA is the OpenTOSCA ecosystem [116] depicted in Fig. 5.31.

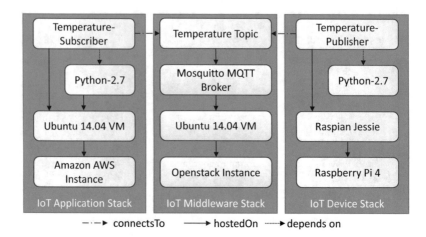

Fig. 5.29 Example of a TOSCA topology for the IoT (based on Franco da Silva et al. [86])

Fig. 5.30 Exemplary TOSCA build plan

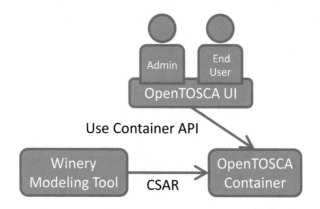

Fig. 5.31 Overview of the OpenTOSCA eco system

OpenTOSCA offers the OpenTOSCA UI, which allows administrators to add new TOSCA based applications and end users to create instances of these applications (assuming a corresponding TOSCA topology has been provided earlier).

On instantiation of a TOSCA topology, the OpenTOSCA UI accesses the so-called OpenTOSCA container, which is responsible for parsing the CSAR and executing the TOSCA build plan. The modeling tool Winery enables modeling

TOSCA topologies and providing the resulting CSARs to the OpenTOSCA container.

OpenTOSCA is open-source and available on Github.[15]

5.7 IoT Application Execution and Monitoring

After IoT software deployment, in the next step of our lifecycle method, the different distributed software components are executed and it needs to be ensured that they can interchange data and they can keep running in a robust and reliable manner, i.e., remain stable even though one of the involved IoT devices might fail.

5.7.1 Execution and Message Exchange

After deployment, message exchange between the different distributed components need to be handled. To do so, Del Gaudio et al. [84] introduce a lightweight *messaging engine*, suitable for the IoT. The overall goal is that different devices can communicate with each other in a highly distributed manner. How the devices can be accessed and which devices communicate with each other has already been defined in an earlier step using the TDLIoT as well as the introduced data processing model.

Figure 5.32 shows on overview of the architecture of this messaging engine. As can be seen, although we aim for a purely distributed environment, there still is a central management component (see right in Fig. 5.32), which is mostly responsible for monitoring and adaptation tasks. Communication is conducted between IoT devices as shown in the architecture on the left.

The idea of this approach is that each IoT device is equipped with a messaging engine, which can be implemented in different programming languages depending on the device. Message exchange is done through standard protocols so the communication can be independent on the concrete implementation of the messaging engine. Traditional message exchange systems, e.g., using SOAP [91], tend to be too heavyweight, thus, Del Gaudio et al. aim for a more lightweight approach.

The communication is done through message queues, whereas each messaging engine contains a message consumer and a message producer queue. These queues are processed by default in a First-in-First-Out fashion but can also be work in a way that certain message are prioritized. Regarding Quality of Service, each message needs to be annotated whether it should arrive exactly one time, at least one time, or at most one time. The queues are then connected to the Message Manager, which serves as a middleware layer between the IoT application logic

---

[15] https://github.com/OpenTOSCA.

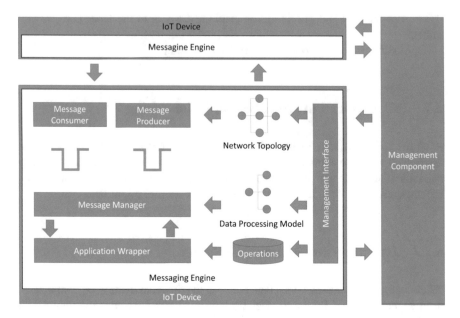

Fig. 5.32 Architecture of the messaging engine (based on Del Gaudio et al. [84])

and the communication through the queues. The IoT application is then provided a software library that can be used to exchange messages.

In order to know which other devices or middleware components exist in the IoT environment, a network topology is given to each IoT device that contains all other devices that can be communicated with. Furthermore, the data processing model describes where the data is coming from and, more importantly, where it needs to be sent next. The network topology and the data processing model can be updated regularly by the Management Interface, communicating with the Management Component.

Now, we assume that each IoT device has been equipped with the introduced messaging engine in the deployment step of our lifecycle together with the application logic which is dependent on the devices and the involved use cases. Then, the messaging engine can be used for communication between the distributed devices by using the built-in means.

Figure 5.33 shows a possible implementation of the messaging engine as introduced by Del Gaudio et al. [84]. In their implementation, CoAP [90] is used for communication between the devices, implemented in Python. Hence, the Python library CoAPthon [92] was used to implemented a CoAP server and client.

Furthermore, the lightweight database ZODB was used to store the messages of the queues. The business logic could then, for example, be implemented using a Python implementation or using an implementation in any other programming language.

Fig. 5.33 Implementation technologies of the messaging engine (based on Del Gaudio et al. [84])

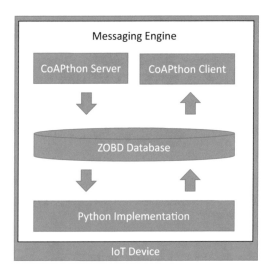

5.8 Monitoring of IoT Applications

Monitoring is a difficult task when it comes to IoT applications since their distributed and heterogeneous manner. Furthermore, using specific monitoring systems can lead to a vendor lock-in, since monitoring systems usually require installing specific agents onto the IoT devices and changing them is difficult afterwards. For this reason, Mormul et al. [93] introduce a model-based approach to avoid this vendor lock-in by using generic monitoring agent templates. Agents are modeled only once in an abstract and generic way and domain experts provide the transformation logic required to transform these agents into executable agents for specific monitoring systems. Therefore, the complexity and time needed to replace a monitoring system are heavily reduced, which also reduces monetary losses. Furthermore, an extended lifecycle for agents is introduced to support their management and automatic deployment.

5.8.1 Generic Agent Templates

By introducing generic agent templates (Fig. 5.34, right), the system administrator only has to model this underlying task once in a generic way. However, those generic agents are non-executable and need to be transformed into a solution-specific agent that is used within the specific company. Because generic agents conform a predefined schema, domain experts with detailed technical knowledge about the several solution-specific agents can provide the transformation logic to transform generic agents into executable agents for the desired monitoring system.

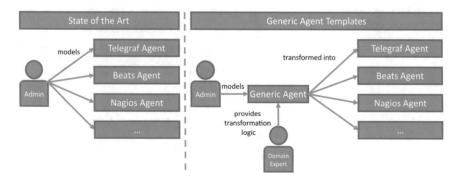

Fig. 5.34 Left: Admin has to model n agents; Right: admin only has to model one agent (based on Mormul et al. [93])

The transformation logic can be shared across all companies and, therefore, only needs to be provided once per supported agent.

To further support system administrators, Mormul et al. [93] introduce an extended lifecycle for agents, as shown in Fig. 5.35. On the left, the current, inadequate lifecycle is shown consisting of two manual tasks *Modeling* and *Manual Deployment*, both performed by system administrators. Each time an agent is modeled or changed, the deployment onto each device must be repeated. To cope with the issues of this approach, Mormul et al. [93] introduce an extended life cycle as shown in Fig. 5.35 (right), which comprises of the following four phases:

- *Phase 1: Modeling:* The demand for genericity and usability requires changes in the modeling phase. We introduce *generic agent templates* to create an abstraction layer that is generic and supports an easy modeling of agents that can be used for multiple monitoring systems.
- *Phase 2: Transformation:* Since the modeled agents are generic and non-executable, the generic agents are transformed into executable, solution-specific agents. To not further burden the system administrator, this task is automated since domain experts provide the transformation logic.
- *Phase 3: Automatic Deployment:* Instead of deploying agents manually, we automate the deployment to tackle scalability issues in large-scale cloud environments using standards-compliant technologies.
- *Phase 4: Adaptation:* We present an agent management to support adaptation of agents to the dynamically changing environment at runtime.

Phase 1: Modeling In general, agents are integrated into specific monitoring systems and cannot be used for different monitoring systems. There are a few exceptions, e.g., Nagios' NRPE agent, which, due to its wide distribution, is supported by many different monitoring systems. However, there are no agents that can be used in all monitoring systems. Also, each agent differs in its syntax, used programming language, and functionality. To enable genericity, Mormul et al. [93]

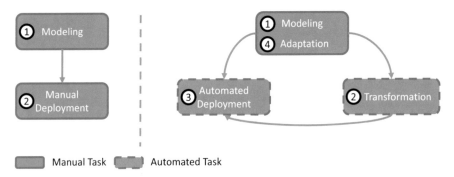

Fig. 5.35 Left: Current agent lifecycle; Right: New, extended agent lifecycle

introduce the novel concept of *generic agent templates* to achieve an abstraction layer for the modeling of agents.

The basis of a generic agent template is the agent pipeline containing the four components *Input, Processor, Aggregator*, and *Output* nodes as shown in Fig. 5.36. This pipeline is based on the plugin-based architecture of agents, e.g., *Telegraf* [94] (TICK-Stack) or *Beats* [95] (ELK-Stack) and enables modeling a flexible and extendable agent due to its modular structure. With those components, a system administrator can model generic agents (exemplary configuration in Fig. 5.37) that can be transformed by the *Agent Mapper* to solution-specific agents. In the following, we describe the nodes and pipeline concept in detail.

- **Input Node** defines what metric the agent is collecting (e.g., *CPU load*). Besides meta data, such as *ID* and *name* of the node, for each input node, the sampling frequency can be set individually, e.g., *CPU load* is collected every second whereas *RAM load* is collected every ten seconds. Data from the Input Node can be sent to *Processor* and *Aggregator* nodes for further processing, or directly to an *Output Node*. A single agent can contain multiple Input Nodes.
- **Processor Node** is an optional node which contains functions that can be executed on single data samples. Examples are transformations of data (e.g., UNIX date to human readable date) or filtering (e.g., $if\ value < 200\,\text{MB}$). At the end, a data sample that passes a Processor Node may receive a tag that may be used for further routing inside the agent pipeline. Based on those tags, data are sent to Aggregator Nodes or Output Nodes.
- **Aggregator Node** is an optional node and acts similar to a Processor Node. The difference is that functions are not performed on single data samples, but on a set of data samples. Therefore, a window is defined, in which the Aggregator Node calculates statistics, e.g., calculate the mean CPU and RAM load over one minute. Again, tags can be added for further routing and data can be sent to Processor Nodes or Output Nodes.

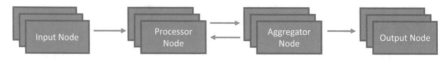

Fig. 5.36 Agent pipeline

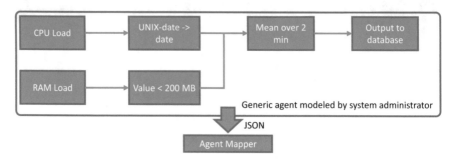

Fig. 5.37 Exemplary generic agent configuration sent to Agent Mapper

- **Output Node** represents the endpoint of a pipeline and defines where data are
  sent to from an agent's perspective (e.g., to a database). Multiple Output Nodes
  can exist and can be chosen based on tags added to the data.

The result of the modeling process is a generic agent in form of a JSON
document. Mormul et al. [93] define a schema[16] for the node definitions using JSON
schema. A small excerpt of this schema for the input node is shown in Listing 5.5.
The *id* is used as an identifier within an agent template. The *type* denotes the type
of input node referring to premodeled input types like CPU input or RAM input.
The *config* contains configurable parameters of the input node, such as sampling
frequency. Finally, *next* describes the next node within the pipeline. Based on this
schema, Mormul et al. [93] implemented a graphical, web-based modeling tool[17]
to ease the modeling and alteration of agents without the need to understand all the
specifics of a monitoring system.

Phase 2: Transformation The result of a modeled agent pipeline is a generic
agent template. The *Agent Mapper* is the component that receives this generic agent
template and transforms it into an executable agent for a specific monitoring system.
Of course, for each supported monitoring system, the transformation logic must
be implemented. Therefore, the complexity and variance of different monitoring
systems is not diminished but rather shifted from the end user to a few domain

---

[16] Generic Agent JSON Schema: https://github.com/mormulms/agent-centric-monitoring/blob/
master/generic-agent/mona-template-editor/src/assets/schema.json.

[17] Agent Modeling Tool: https://github.com/mormulms/agent-centric-monitoring/blob/master/
generic-agent/mona-template-editor.

```
"GenericInput": {
    "type": "object",
    "properties": {
      "id": {
        "$ref": "#/definitions/InputId"
      },
      "type": {
        "$ref": "#/definitions/NodeType"
      },
      "config": {
        "$ref": "#/definitions/InputConfig"
      },
      "next": {
        "$ref": "#/definitions/NextArray"
      }
    },
    ...
}
```

Listing 5.5 Excerpt of the input node definition

experts who implement the transformation logic for specific monitoring agents. Those implementations must be shared publicly to gain an advantage. So far, in our current prototype, we only support transformations to Telegraf. To support further monitoring systems and agents in the future, we created an extendable, modular architecture for the Agent Mapper. Agents, such as Telegraf, already have the functionalities for processing and aggregating monitoring data and, therefore, are simple to transform to. However, agents that do not support one or more of those functionalities require a more complicated transformation. The most basic agent always has a means to collect data and send it to the destination, i.e., the monitoring server. However, if a modeled generic agent contains functionality such as aggregation and the system administrator wants to transform this generic agent into a solution-specific agent that does not support this functionality, there are two options: (i) the system administrator receives a warning that the transformation is not possible and needs to select a different solution-specific agent, which the generic agent should be transformed into. The second option is the use of a Complex Event Processing (CEP) engine or similar engines. The agent sends its collected monitoring data to this engine. Then, the processing and/or aggregation nodes can be translated into CEP queries to perform the needed functionalities and forward the monitoring data back to the agent which further forwards it to the monitoring server. This greatly increases the impact of generic agents since a transformation to many existing monitoring agents is possible.

Phase 3: Automatic Deployment Especially in large-scaled scenarios with a large number of VMs, any manual task becomes cumbersome, error-prone, and simply does not scale. Therefore, an automatic deployment is essential [96, 97]. There are many existing tools and platforms for automated deployment, such as *Docker* [99] or *Vagrant* [98]. A few monitoring systems like *Splunk* [100] support this feature as well. However, a standardized deployment framework is desirable, since technologies tend to disappear over time.

An established deployment standard is the Topology and Orchestration Specification for Cloud Applications (*TOSCA*) [6] of the Organization for the Advancement of Structured Information Standards (*OASIS*). TOSCA enables a two-step software deployment approach. First, a topology template is created, modeling the application, platform, and infrastructure components. Second, this topology is used to deploy the components in the corresponding infrastructure.

One implementation of the TOSCA standard is OpenTOSCA [101]. OpenTOSCA provides an eco system consisting of the TOSCA topology modeler Winery [102], the OpenTOSCA container that handles the actual software deployment based on the topology, and a self-service portal called Vinothek [103]. TOSCA and its implementation OpenTOSCA can be used in our approach for automated deployment of monitoring agents. Since TOSCA is a standard, it provides a high degree of applicability and is future-secure.

Mormul et al. [93] modeled a topology template using OpenTOSCA to deploy a monitoring system and a template to deploy agents. If a new virtual machine is started, an agent is deployed on it to guarantee a monitoring from the beginning.

Phase 4: Adaption According to Gartner [104], flexibility against a changing IT architecture is a key objective when investing in new monitoring systems. The modeling of agents is influenced by the current business needs and the status of the current cloud environment. However, both of these variables may change over time. In this case, starting a new agent life cycle is excessive when only minor changes to the agent are required. Instead, the user should be able to access the previously modeled generic agents and change them to fit the current needs. The changes are then propagated to all agents originating from this generic agent. To support this process, we implemented a prototype as shown in Fig. 5.38. The user models a new generic agent or changes an existing one via the web-based modeling tool, which is connected to the *Deployment Server* on the *Monitoring Server*. The deployment server is responsible for the management of the generic agents, which are stored in the *Generic Agent Database*. On the virtual machines, a *Deployment Agent* periodically requests the configuration (the transformed generic agent) for the agent and resolves differences between the retrieved configuration and the currently used one. In case of changed configurations or failures, the deployment agent automatically restarts the agent.

5.8.2 Related Work

The transformation of abstract models to a concrete executable implementation is a commonly used means in order to abstract from technical details. Consequently,

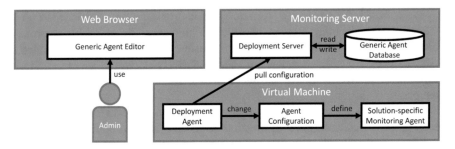

Fig. 5.38 Architecture for automatic adaptations at runtime

domain users are able to create models on a high level of abstraction without requiring technical knowledge about their realization. The use of a single abstract model leads to genericity and reduces the threat of vendor lock-in, since it is not dependent on specific technologies. In the following, approaches are described that aim at a similar approach for transforming abstract models into concrete ones.

Falkenthal et al. [105] aim towards a generic approach to transform abstract pattern languages to concrete solution implementations. Since their approach is generic, they do not focus on a specific domain but rather discuss how such a transformation can be conducted in general. In their work, Mormul et al. apply this approach to the concrete domain of monitoring by introducing a mapping of generic monitoring templates to concrete, executable implementations.

Eilam et al. [106] introduce an approach for model-based provisioning and management of applications. Through transformations, application topologies are mapped onto different levels of abstraction in order to finally create executable implementations that can be deployed. However, Eilam et al. require a premodeling of concrete implementation artifacts, which is not necessary in the approach of Mormul et al..

Furthermore, Eilam et al. introduce a combination of a model-based and workflow-based approach for the automated provisioning of the transformed applications. This approach creates a provisioning model based on workflow technology that can be used for automated deployment. In this paper, we also introduce an approach how the templates can be automatically deployed after transformation, which uses existing software deployment technologies instead of this heavy-weight workflow-based approach.

Similar approaches regarding the agent templates are introduced by Künzle et al. [107] and Cohn et al. [108] that use artifact-centric approaches. In these approaches, so-called business artifacts are created, i.e., abstract representations of software components with the goal of hiding technical details. These artifacts can be mapped onto concrete executable implementations, as shown by Sun et al. [109]. However, the business artifacts of Künzle et al. and Cohn et al. are vaguely described, i.e., only on a conceptual level, an example application is missing. Mormul et al. introduce a concrete scenario our concepts can be applied to.

Reimann [110] introduces generic patterns for simulation workflows that are also mapped onto concrete executable implementations, in his approach onto workflow fragments provided in the Business Process Execution Language (BPEL) [72]. However, Reimann focuses exclusively on workflows. In contrast, Mormul et al. focus on agents and model their capabilities through tailored templates.

In our previous work [111], we introduced so-called Situation Templates, which represent abstract descriptions of situations to be recognized without the necessity to provide technical implementation details. These situation templates can be mapped onto various formats, for example, complex event processing queries. Mormul et al. adapt this concept to the domain of cloud monitoring to make it suitable for modeling of agents.

5.8.3   Conclusion

The monitoring of complex cloud environments can lead to several challenges. Selecting an unsuitable monitoring system or evolving business needs may lead to a required replacement of the monitoring system. However, monitoring agents are spread across the IT environment and, oftentimes, can be tightly integrated into the monitoring system. Therefore, the replacement of the agents is a time-consuming task and the modeling of new agents requires technical expertise. For this, Mormul et al. [93] introduce generic agent templates to unburden system administrators by creating an abstraction to the modeling of agents. System administrators model generic agents once and domain experts provide the transformation logic required to transform the generic agents to solution-specific agents. This way, generic agents can be transformed into several solution-specific agents without further additional work. Expressiveness is provided by the agent pipeline consisting of Input, Processor, Aggregator, and Output Nodes. Of each node, multiple instances can be created so that system administrators can model arbitrary agent configurations. Furthermore, if solution-specific agents do not support some of those functionalities, e.g., processing, a transformation to CEP queries is also possible to even support agents with missing functionalities. Lastly, an extended life cycle supports management, automatic deployment, and adaptation of agents at runtime using state-of-the-art and standardized technologies. Transformations to solution-specific agents are automated via the Agent Mapper. The automatic deployment is enabled using the deployment standard TOSCA. Adaptations to generic agents at runtime are automatically propagated to all according agents.

5.9 IoT Application Adaptation

The next step of our lifecycle is the adaptation of IoT applications. Adaptation needs to occur if a new IoT device enters the environment, a device is being retired or fails unexpectedly. Hence, we do need a means to cope with such situations.

Our goal is that IoT applications are able to include newly appearing devices or to cope with leaving or failing devices automatically with minimal human interaction. To realize this, in this chapter, we introduce a method, introduced by Del Gaudio et al. [84], for device management in IoT environments by providing seamless integration of devices. The approach includes (i) using the previously introduced IoT environment models and IoT data processing models that describe the structure and behavior of an IoT environment, (ii) a life cycle method to integrate new devices into existing IoT environments regarding their capabilities and the environment's requirements, and (iii) a system architecture to implement the method. The approach is evaluated through a prototypical implementation of this architecture.

One important aspect of this work is keeping everything as decentralized as possible. More precisely, the number of central components should be kept as low as possible since the vision of the IoT focuses mainly on direct machine-to-machine communication.

5.9.1 Used Models

As mentioned before, we use two models as the foundation for the seamless integration of IoT devices: (i) the introduced data processing model (Sect. 5.5.2), specifying the data flow of an application, and (ii) a structural description of smart factory environments, including devices, sensors, actuators, network, and communication, which is similar to the ones introduced in Sect. 5.2.

As mentioned before, using such a model based approach enables decoupling of data processing from the actual physical devices that execute data processing operations. This leads to a clear separation of concerns. Hence, devices can be added, removed, and exchanged without having to adapt the data processing model, which can lead to the desired adaptation in this step of our lifecycle method. Furthermore, an application developer can model an IoT application's data flow via the data processing model without further knowledge of the structure of the IoT environment in which the application will be executed. Consequently, both models are also fully decoupled and, thus, interchangeable. The data processing model has already been introduced in Sect. 5.5.2. In the following, we describe the used IoT environment model for this approach, which is a simplified model to enhance comprehensibility.

5.9.1.1 Used IoT Environment Model

Additionally to the behavior of the applications, we need a model to specify the structure of the underlying IoT environment, the *IoT environment model* as introduced in Sect. 5.2. This model describes all included devices in the environment and the connections between them. For a simplified model to be used in this adaptation approach, we propose an undirected and weighted graph $E = (D, L, C, cap, w)$ with a set of devices $D = \{d_1, \dots, d_n\}$, that exist in the environment, a set of links $L = \{l = \{d_i, d_j\}|d_i, d_j \in D\}$, stating that device d_i can communicate with device d_j and vice versa, and a set of capabilities C. The function $cap : D \to \mathcal{P}(C)$ links each device with a set of capabilities in order to match them with the requirements of the processing model. The function $w :\to \mathbb{Q}$ associates each link with a specific weight. The weight of a link indicates the costs of delivering a message via the link. The weight of a link can be very dynamic and must be monitored during runtime.

The environment model needs to be changed by devices being added and removed, which is the main contribution of this work. This model in JSON representation is shown in the following example:

```
{
  "devices": [
    {
      "address": "192.168.56.11",
      "capabilities": [
        "AccelerationController",
        "PositionSensor",
        "LowProcessingPower",
        "Forklift"
        ],
        "credentialGroup": "group1",
        "mac": "f0-f4-85-f5-41-e6-53",
        "name": "SmartForklift"
    },
    {
      "address": "192.168.56.22",
      "capabilities": [
        "GateController",
        "LightBarrier"
        ],
        "credentialGroup": "group1",
        "mac": "00-53-b7-ff-21-24-34",
        "name": "SmartGate"
    }
    ],
    "link_1_2": {
      "devices": [
        "SmartForklift",
        "SmartGate"
        ],
        "weight": 2.3
    }
}
```

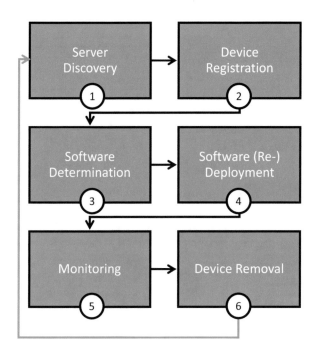

Fig. 5.39 Life cycle to seamlessly integrate IoT devices (based on [112])

This example defines an excerpt of the involved devices of our Industry 4.0 scenario introduced in Sect. 3.1 including one of the forklifts as well as an automated gate. Note that links in the environment model are not necessary in smart factory environments where every device is able to connect to every other device via a network and link costs are not relevant. Furthermore, especially in environments with mobile devices, link costs are highly dynamic.

5.9.2 Lifecycle Method for Seamless Integration of IoT Devices

In their work, Del Gaudio et al. [113] propose a generic life cycle method with six steps to integrate a new device into an existing IoT environment, which is depicted in Fig. 5.39 [112]. The life cycle method describes how one device can be integrated into an existing IoT environment to work together with the other devices. It describes the cycle of entering, leaving, and reentering of a single device in an IoT environment. Furthermore, Del Gaudio et al. [113] propose a system architecture that implements the life cycle, which is depicted in Fig. 5.40.

The cycle is started by the *runtime agent* (cf. Fig. 5.40) on the device discovering the *runtime management*, representing our system for device integration (step 1). In the second step, the device can register itself at an registration service

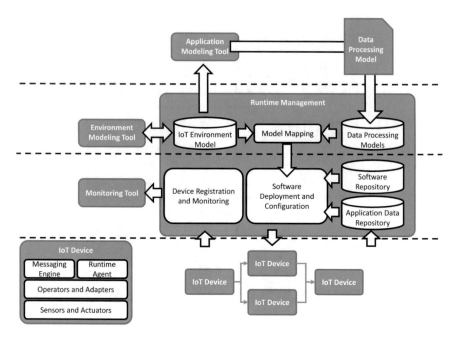

Fig. 5.40 Architecture to apply our life cycle method for device integration (based on Del Gaudio et al. [113])

by sending a *registration message*. The registration service fills the *environment model database* with the following data: (i) information about each device that is registered, (ii) information about each operation that can potentially be deployed and executed in the environment, and (iii) information about which operation is deployed on which device.

In the next step, the *model mapping* component of the runtime management determines the proper set of operations to deploy on the new device, as defined by the processing model of the IoT application stored inside the *processing model repository* (step 3) and created by the *application designer* using the *application modelling tool*. After that, the *software deployment and configuration* component deploys the associated software and configures it using the designated processing models and the software from the *software repository* (step 4). If the device has been a part of the environment in the past and has stored data in the *application data repository*, the data is also transferred back to the device, so that is can resume processing it at the point that it left the environment.

The next step 5 represents the data processing, i.e., including the new device into the execution of the running processing models of the IoT environment. The runtime management is now only responsible for monitoring the new device and is not involved in the machine-to-machine coordination. Hence, decentralized data processing can still be ensured, which improves the robustness due to no single point of failure. Finally, in the last step 6 of our life cycle method, the device is removed from the environment, either intentionally or by failure.

The details of these steps are described in the following sections.

5.9.2.1 Step 1: Server Discovery

The first step of our life cycle method is the server discovery. In order for a device to be integrated in an IoT application, it must register itself at the device registration and monitoring component, i.e., the registration server.

Del Gaudio et al. evaluated three possibilities how a device can find the registration server in a network: (i) the address of the registration component is preconfigured on the device, (ii) the device sends a broadcast or multicast message into the network hoping that the registration server receives it and sends a response, or (iii) the server discovery is implemented into the network via a DHCP or DNS server.

Del Gaudio et al. do not further consider the first solution, since preconfiguration of devices omits the dynamicity they aim for. For example, when a device enters a different environment, the address of the registration server might be different than the one that is preconfigured. Furthermore, the address of the registration server could change anytime.

The third solution requires specifically configured DNS or DHCP servers and is, thus, also not further regarded. Consequently, Del Gaudio et al. prefer the second solution, since it can be implemented by our system itself without any critical dependencies. The runtime agent on the devices sends broadcast messages into the network and the registration server responds on receiving the message. If the network does not allow broadcasting, the other solutions can be considered as a backup. In the introduced forklift scenario, the registration server is represented by the Road Side Unit, the trucks and forklifts communicate with once they enter the environment.

5.9.2.2 Step 2: Device Registration

The second step of the life cycle method comprises the device registration. After a new device discovered the address of the registration server (step 1), it registers itself by sending a *registration message* to the registration server. An example of such a message for the given motivating scenario is depicted in the following, in which the truck registers itself on arrival:

```
{
    "device": {
        "name": "SmartTruck",
        "capabilities": [
            "AccelerationController",
            "PositionSensor",
```

```
            "HighProcessingPower"
        ],
        "address": "192.168.56.11",
        "mac": "12-43-b5-ae-fd-44-35",
        "credentialGroup": "group2"
    },
    "options": {
        "ttl": 3600
    }
}
```

The element `device` defines device-specific metadata. `name` is the self-given name for the device that does not necessarily have to be unique. The subelement `capabilities` is used to choose appropriate operations for the device, `address` defines the IP address, `mac` the MAC address, and `credentialGroup` is used to define the credentials to access the device, for example, via SSH. Furthermore, the element `options` is used for the registration process itself, defining important properties, such as `ttl`, determining the time-to-life for the registration as explained in Sect. 5.9.2.5. The registration server stores the information about the device based on the registration message. After step 2, the device is registered and can be further processed.

5.9.2.3 Step 3: Software Determination

As the device is registered at the registration server, the server must now determine a suitable set of operations, implementing specific business logic of the IoT application (for example, delivering goods from one location to another), and deploy them on the device. This is done in step 3 of the life cycle method.

Del Gaudio et al. determined three aspects to consider for choosing suitable operations: (i) the capabilities of the device in terms of sensors, actuators, and processing power, (ii) the requirements of available operations in terms of sensors, actuators, and processing power, and (iii) the specific characteristics of the environment the IoT applications are provided in.

In the architecture (cf. Fig. 5.40), the *Model Mapping* component is responsible to map the capabilities of the devices onto the most useful set of applications, regarding all applications that are available in the software repository.

Del Gaudio et al. define the function $fulfills(c, r)$ for each requirement $r \in R$ and each capability $c \in C$, which evaluates to 1 if capability c fulfills requirement r. Therefore, Del Gaudio et al. define the function $executableBy(o, d)$ for each operation $o \in O$ and each device $d \in D$ as

$$executableBy(o, d) = \begin{cases} 1, & \forall r \in req(o) \exists c \in cap(d): \\ & fulfills(c, r) = 1 \\ 0, & else \end{cases} \tag{5.1}$$

stating that o is executable by d in terms that for each of requirement d, o offers a fulfilling capability.

For a new device d, we can now seek for the subset of operations

$$O_d = \{o \in O | executableBy(o, d) = 1\}, \tag{5.2}$$

which contains all operations that are executable by d and, thus, fulfills aspects (i) and (ii).

In terms of aspect (iii), many different characteristics must be considered when choosing which operation is the most "useful" for an environment. Del Gaudio et al. consider an operation as the most useful for an environment if it is one that is not yet deployed on a device at all, expanding the application's coverage of the IoT environment.

Furthermore, for choosing suitable operations to be run of the devices, Del Gaudio et al. evaluated two processing patterns that need to be handled separately:

- **Parallelizable operations:**
  Parallelizable operations can be scaled horizontally by deploying multiple instances of them. Hence, when deploying such operations, it needs to be considered whether scaling is required by the specific application. Furthermore, if all available operations are already deployed, only parallelizable operations are considered.
- **Unique operations:**
  A unique operation must be unique inside the environment, for example, because all data that is processed by the operation must be consolidated in one instance. Unique operations must be considered separately when choosing the operations to be deployed.

To manage the operations in the environment, we must keep track of operations that are already running, the workload of each operation, and the utilization of resources of the devices. The set of operations that are executed by a given device d in the context of any processing model is determined by $executedBy(d)$. In order to realize this, a sophisticated monitoring of the environment is essential. However, this is not the focus of this work. Hence, we refer to existing work in monitoring, for example, provided by Lazarescu [114], that can be implemented in the runtime agent and the device registration and monitoring component.

5.9.2.4 Step 4: Software Deployment and Configuration

In the fourth step, the chosen operations need to be deployed on the new device. For each operation the environment is able to perform, the associated software components must be stored in the *software repository* which is part of the runtime management, as shown in the system architecture (cf. Fig. 5.40). These software components can range from simple scripts to sophisticated software applications, whereas only lightweight components can be deployed onto resource-restricted hardware. This decision has already been made in the previous step Software Determination.

The Software Deployment component of our architecture extracts the necessary software components from the software repository, connects to the device, and starts installing the software and all required dependencies. This deployment step can be either implemented manually using, for example, SSH connections, or in a more sophisticated manner. As introduced before, one approach for a more robust software deployment strategy is offered by the OASIS standard TOSCA [88, 115]. An open-source implementation of TOSCA is, for example, provided by OpenTOSCA [116]. By using a standard-based approach, such as TOSCA, the deployment strategy is more future-proof than a non-standard-based approach.

After all applications have been deployed, the messaging engine on the devices (responsible for machine-to-machine communication) must be configured accordingly (cf. Sect. 5.7.1). The messaging engine needs the operations it can perform, the section of the processing model it participates in, and the node information of devices it must interact with.

Furthermore, messaging engines on other devices that need to interact with the new devices need the information about the newly appeared device, more specifically, which operations it provides and how they can interact with it. A simpler but less scalable solution would be to inform each device in the environment about the newly appeared device (for example, through broadcasting) and, in this process, hand over the necessary information about the new device. However, since devices of IoT environments often tend to be constrained in terms of memory capacity and to minimize network traffic, we do not consider this simple solution.

In this approach, to compute all relevant devices that need to communicate with a newly added device d, the runtime management traverses the processing model and looks for each operation in $executedBy(d)$. Every device that executes a predecessor of an operation in $executedBy(d)$ must be notified about d. Vice versa, d must be notified about each device, that executes a successor operation of each operation in $executedBy(o)$. By doing so, only the devices need to be notified, which are required to interact with the newly added device. This reduces the network traffic that would have been produced by broadcast messages and leads to a more tailored solution.

Note that devices can also communicate using MQTT [83]. Therefore, the software deployment and configuration component would deploy MQTT clients and brokers on devices and configure them in the same manner as the messaging engine.

5.9.2.5 Step 5: Data Processing and Monitoring

After deployment of the required software components, the newly added device is ready to process data. It can receive, process, and forward data according to the processing models. The system is now also able to monitor the devices in the environment. To realize this, each runtime agent sends health messages to the server periodically. The frequency highly depends on the use case, i.e., how critical device failures influence the health of the application.

When the server receives no health message from a device for a specified period of time, it assumes that the device has left the environment accidentally, for example, due to an occurring device failure. In case the device leaves the environment voluntarily, it deregisters itself. This will be discussed in more depth in step 6. The time period is specified in `ttl` in `options` in the registration message as introduced in Sect. 5.9.2.2. This time period can be individual for each device, since IoT environments tend to be highly heterogeneous. In order to prevent unnecessary network traffic, choosing the right time period in which devices send their heartbeat messages has to be considered wisely.

Furthermore, for device health monitoring, important metrics are the weight of links (cf. Sect. 5.9.1) and the resource utilization of devices. Monitoring information can be used to detect bottlenecks and react accordingly, for example, by deploying additional software on devices in order to scale the application.

When the data processing is interrupted because a device is not capable of finding an appropriate receiver for data, it can perform a request to the device registration and monitoring component, which will then respond by adjusting the environment model which triggers the model mapping component and, thus, the reconfiguration of the device with the address of another device hosting the desired operation or deploy the operation on one.

5.9.2.6   Step 6: Device Removal

There are two ways a device is removed from the environment: on purpose, for example, when a smart truck in our introduced scenario leaves the smart factory area, or accidentally, for example, when the network connection is lost or when the device's hardware fails.

When a device leaves the environment on purpose, e.g., when it should be exchanged, it should be able to backup all its data in the *application data repository* in the runtime management depicted in Fig. 5.40. When a new device enters the environment that is able to perform one of the operations the leaving device performed, the runtime management can initialize the new device with the backup data. By doing so, it can be ensured that no data is left. Of course, this data needs to be attached with a timespan until it gets stale. Especially streaming data get stale very quickly, thus, loses its usefulness after a short amount of time.

When a device leaves the environment accidentally, loss of data can only be prevented by persistently storing all data on the device hoping that it reenters. If this is not the case, however, all data that was stored on the device at the time of the failure is lost. One solution to cope with this issue are periodical backups in the application data repository. However, it needs to be considered that these backups lead to a significant overhead regarding computing and network resources. Hence, this trade-off needs to be carefully considered for each application separately.

After the last step of our life cycle method, the device leaves the environment. At any time, the device can re-enter and the whole method is re-initialized by using associated data in the application data repository. Note that if a device already contains the required software components when re-entering, the method can be significantly accelerated. Thus, it also considers previous iterations.

5.9.3   Related Work

In Sect. 5.7.1, we introduced a lightweight messaging engine to enable device-to-device communication. This messaging engine handles information exchange between devices in a dynamic, scalable, and robust manner. Data processing is defined by a processing model. Data is exchanged in the form of messages containing a header and a payload with the actual data. In this previous work, the messaging engine still lacks mechanisms to cope with the dynamic we aim for in this paper. Hence, in this work, Del Gaudio et al. enhance this messaging engine so it can cope with newly added or failing devices and enable a more dynamic device-to-device communication.

Seeger et al. [117] propose an approach to process data in Industry 4.0 environments in a distributed manner, which is similar to the one of Del Gaudio et al. They model data processing based on choreographies [118]. They also introduce a concept for failure detection, where devices monitor themselves to detect failures. In contrast to our work, Seeger et al. specifically focus on device failures and their recovery in the scope of their choreographies. Newly appearing devices, however, are not discovered and considered automatically. Moreover, Del Gaudio et al. aim at creating a more generic approach, which is not only valid specifically for choreographies but for all kinds of models.

Franco da Silva et al. [119, 120] propose the new IoT platform MBP as well as means to map operators onto distributed IoT devices and execute them. However, they do not provide any mechanisms for coping with newly appearing devices or device failures.

Kodeswaran et al. [122] introduce Idea—a system for efficient failure management in smart IoT environments. The core of the Idea approach is a central system, which provides means for monitoring failures of sensors and, if a failure occurs, a scheduling component for maintenance. The work focuses mostly on Smart Home applications. In contrast to Kodeswaran et al., Del Gaudio et al. do not only cope with failing devices but also integrate new devices into the IoT applications. Furthermore, their approach is more decentralized, whereas the Idea framework describes a central system.

Similar to Kodeswaran et al. [122], Kapitanova et al. [121] introduce a system to handle non-stopping failures in Smart Home environments. Failure detection is done by machine learning algorithms. In contrast, Del Gaudio et al. aim at a more traditional, lightweight monitoring approach and, furthermore, they also provide means to handle newly added devices, not only the ones that fail.

Very similar to this approach is the research area of discovery in the IoT. Datta et al. [123] categorize related work in the area of discovery into the following areas: distributed and peer-to-peer discovery services, centralized architectures, CoAP-based service discovery, semantic-based discovery, search engines for resource directory, and utilization of ONS and DNS.

Fredj et al. [125] propose a semantic-based service discovery using ontologies. A semantic model that can be used to achieve discovery in such a manner is IoT-Lite [124]. Del Gaudio et al. use a similar, however, more lightweight approach that introduces a meta model that represents the IoT devices of an application that is used for discovery purposes. By doing so, discovery can be enabled more efficiently in contrast to working with heavyweight ontology models.

CoAP-based discovery mechanisms can make use of the resource discovery (/.well-known/core) interface of a CoAP server, through which provided services of the server can be retrieved [126, 127]. Cirani et al. [128] propose an architecture for peer-to-peer-based autonomous resource and service discovery in the IoT. The architecture utilizes a central IoT gateway and the CoAP resource discovery interface. In their work, Del Gaudio et al. decided to focus on a more generic approach for device discovery and integration that is not specifically tailored to CoAP.

The W3C Web of Things Working Group[18] introduces an architecture and a description language for things. Furthermore, in the scope of the W3C Web of Things Working Group, Sciullo et al. [129] propose a store to discover and deploy software for IoT devices. In contrast to the W3C solutions, Del Gaudio et al. aim to minimize communication with devices and central management components. Software and application logic is deployed once on devices so that devices can interact autonomously and only communicate directly with each other.

There are also proprietary solutions, e.g., by Google[19] or Microsoft.[20] Del Gaudio et al. aim to create a solution to deploy software and processes in IoT environments independent from specific vendors or software distributors. A possible next step would be to integrate such proprietary solutions into their concept.

In conclusion, the thorough literature review of related work shows that even though there are already many works focusing either on device failures or on device discovery and integration, there is yet no combined approach, which provides the flexibility, dynamics and genericity that Del Gaudio et al. provides.

---

[18] https://www.w3.org/WoT/.

[19] https://cloud.google.com/solutions/iot.

[20] https://azure.microsoft.com/overview/iot/.

5.9.4   Prototype and Discussion

To evaluate the concept, Del Gaudio et al. [113] implemented a prototype of the runtime management and the runtime agent, running on the device itself (cf. Fig. 5.40).

The agent application is implemented in Python to guarantee a certain degree of lightweightness because this agent is usually deployed onto resource-limited IoT hardware. In contrast, the runtime management components, running in a scalable cloud environment, is implemented in Java.

These components communicate via CoAP, a lightweight HTTP-like protocol. In order to implement the CoAP client and server applications, Del Gaudio et al. used the Python implementation CoAPthon [92] for the client and the Java implementation Californium [130] for the server. Furthermore, Del Gaudio et al. use MongoDB[21] as database to store information about registered devices on the server. In addition, all communication payload is serialized in JSON.

Del Gaudio et al. evaluated their prototype at one of Germanys largest producer of forklifts and other transport vehicles. As a platform for the registration server, Del Gaudio et al. use an Industrial Edge Cloud solution, which runs the Linux distribution Redhat.

As devices, a forklift, an automated door, as well as batteries are used, whereas the batteries are the goods to be transported by the forklift. The forklift and door are equipped with an device that provides computing power, storage, and network communication through WiFi or LTE. Route computing of the forklifts are done on the attached device itself, communication between the forklifts is done through LTE.

The runtime management component is set up in the Industial Edge Cloud. In order to set this component, a few simple steps need to be conducted, thus, making it easy to set it up in different scenarios by different stakeholders. First the runtime management needs to be deployed on the Industrial Edge Cloud, manually or over-the-air. Second, the runtime agent must be installed on each device that is involved in the scenario, i.e., the attached devices of forklift and door. Furthermore, each device needs a minor preconfiguration to be able to share its capabilities with the runtime management. For many devices, we recommend automating this installation and configuration step, using for example, TOSCA or other well-known deployment tools, such as Ansible.[22]

As mentioned before, all additional software necessary for a specific scenario should be stored in the software repository and gets installed automatically by the runtime management according to the data processing model for the scenario and the devices capabilities in step 4 of the introduced life cycle method.

---

[21] https://www.mongodb.com.

[22] https://www.ansible.com/.

The prototype shows that the concept can cope with the challenges listed in Sect. 1.1. Devices are automatically registered when they enter the area of our environment and connect to the WiFi (i). Software is automatically deployed on each device according to the processing model (ii). Data is (pre-)processed on the devices by the deployed software and is sent to the other devices according to the data processing and IoT environment models ((iii) and (iv)).

Modelling distributed applications with the data processing model and the IoT environment with the IoT environment model in Sect. 5.9.1.1 decouples application development from executing environments and, thus, creates dynamic IoT environments with interchangeable devices. Data processing can be scaled horizontally by adding more devices to the environment, since parallelizable operations are deployed automatically and load is balanced amongst them. Nonetheless, Del Gaudio et al. did not consider security threats, which will be part of their future work [131, 132].

5.9.5   Conclusion

We described an approach for seamless integration of devices in IoT environments in this chapter, as introduced by Del Gaudio et al. [84]. By introducing a live cycle method, newly appearing devices can be seamlessly integrated into IoT applications without the need for manual, time-consuming steps. In addition, we introduce concepts that allow coping with failing devices or voluntarily leaving ones. Our life cycle method builds on meta models, describing data processing and the infrastructure landscape. Based on these models, newly appearing devices can be found, registered, necessary software can be installed and they can be integrated for data processing in an IoT application. Finally, the device can be retired either voluntarily or when it fails. Even in case of a failure, we can support IoT applications in providing a robust way of data processing so that applications do not fail when single devices do [133].

5.10   IoT Application Retirement

The final step of our life cycle method is the retirement of an IoT application. Retirement usually occurs if the application is not needed anymore or if it is replaced by another application.

In order to retire an IoT application, basically all steps conducted to set it up need to be reversed. First of all, the software components should be retired and removed from the IoT devices.

To realize this, the TOSCA standard provides so-called termination plans, which are basically processes defining which components need to be stopped an uninstalled and in which order. This includes infrastructural components, such as

Fig. 5.41 Exemplary TOSCA build plan

Fig. 5.42 TOSCA termination plan for the build plan example

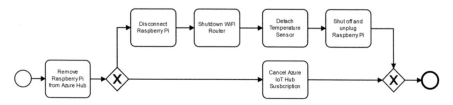

Fig. 5.43 Retirement process for an IoT application

the cancelling of virtual machine subscriptions, platform components, such as web servers, and application components, such as databases. The termination plan can be generated based on the TOSCA build plan, which defines how the components need to be set up. An exemplary TOSCA termination plan for the TOSCA build plan shown in Fig. 5.41 is depicted in Fig. 5.42

After the software components have been retired, the physical hardware needs to be shut down, collected and evaluated for re-use. As introduced in Sect. 5.3, we can use the process models that were defined to set up the IoT environment in order to understand how the components can be shut down and disconnected. Finally, the IoT hardware needs to be collected and it needs to be evaluated whether they can be re-used in another IoT application or whether they can be recycled.

Figure 5.43 shows an example for an uninstalling of the IoT application set up in Fig. 5.23. In this example, the goal was to connect a Raspberry Pi, attached with a temperature sensor, to the Microsoft Azure IoT hub. To retire this IoT application, first, the Raspberry Pi needs to be removed from the Azure IoT Hub. Next, while cancelling the subscription to the IoT hub, assuming that this service is not needed by any other IoT application, the Raspberry Pi needs to be disconnected. That is, the agent connecting to the Azure Cloud needs to be stopped. After that, the used WiFi routed can be disconnected, the temperature sensor can be physically detached and the Raspberry Pi can be shut off. This the concludes the uninstalling of the physical environment.

The retirement step finalized the introduced life cycle method. Once a new application should be developed, the life cycle again starts from the beginning.

References

1. Frigo, M., Hirmer, P., Silva, A., & Thom, L. A. (2020). Toolbox for the internet of things - easing the setup of iot applications. In *ER forum, demo and posters 2020 co-located with 39th international conference on conceptual modeling (ER 2020), Vienna, Austria, November 3–6, 2020* (Vol. 2716, pp. 87–100). http://ceur-ws.org/Vol-2716/paper7.pdf
2. Silva, A., Breitenbücher, U., Hirmer, P., Képes, K., Kopp, O., Leymann, F., Mitschang, B., & Steinke, R. (2017). Internet of things out of the box: Using TOSCA for automating the deployment of IoT environments. In *Proceedings of the 7th international conference on cloud computing and services science (CLOSER)* (pp. 358–367).
3. Structured Information Standards, O. TOSCA Primer. (online, 2013). http://docs.oasis-open.org/tosca/tosca-primer/v1.0/cnd01/tosca-primer-v1.0-cnd01.pdf
4. Yelamarthi, K., Aman, M., & Abdelgawad, A. (2017). An application-driven modular IoT architecture. *Wireless Communications And Mobile Computing, 2017*(1), 1–16.
5. Bermudez-Edo, M., Elsaleh, T., Barnaghi, P., & Taylor, K. (2016). Iot-lite: A lightweight semantic model for the internet of things. In *Ubiquitous intelligence & computing, advanced and trusted computing, scalable computing and communications, cloud and big data computing, internet of people, and smart world congress (UIC/ATC/ScalCom/CBDCom/IoP/Smart-World), 2016 International IEEE Conferences* (pp. 90–97)
6. OASIS Open Topology and Orchestration Specification for Cloud Applications Version 1.0. (2019). Online, http://docs.oasis-open.org/tosca/TOSCA/v1.0/os/TOSCA-v1.0-os.html
7. W3C IoT-Lite Ontology. (2015). Online, https://www.w3.org/Submission/2015/SUBM-iot-lite-20151126, https://www.w3.org/Submission/2015/SUBM-iot-lite-20151126
8. W3C Semantic Sensor Network Ontology. (2005). Online, https://www.w3.org/2005/Incubator/ssn/ssnx/ssn, https://www.w3.org/2005/Incubator/ssn/ssnx/ssn
9. OGC Sensor Model Language (SensorML). (2014). Online, http://www.opengeospatial.org/standards/sensorml, http://www.opengeospatial.org/standards/sensorml
10. Antoniou, G., & Harmelen, F. (2004). Web ontology language: OWL. *Handbook On Ontologies* (pp. 67–92). Springer.
11. Silva, A. & Hirmer, P. (2020). Models for internet of things environments: A survey. *Information, 11*. https://www.mdpi.com/2078-2489/11/10/487
12. Strang, T., & Linnhoff-Popien, C. (2004). A context modeling survey. In *Workshop on advanced context modelling, reasoning and management, UbiComp* (Vol. 4, pp. 34–41).
13. Glaessgen, E., & Stargel, D. (2012). The digital twin paradigm for future NASA and U.S. Air Force vehicles. In *53rd AIAA/ASME/ASCE/AHS/ASC structures, structural dynamics and materials conference*. https://arc.aiaa.org/doi/abs/10.2514/6.2012-1818
14. Boschert, S., & Rosen, R. (2016). Digital twin: The simulation aspect. In *Mechatronic futures: Challenges and solutions for mechatronic systems and their designers* (pp. 59–74).
15. Silva, A., Hirmer, P., & Mitschang, B. (2019). Model-based operator placement for data processing in IoT environments. In *Proceedings of the IEEE international conference on smart computing (SMARTCOMP)*.
16. Guarino, N., Oberle, D., & Staab, S. (2009). What is an ontology? In *Handbook on ontologies* (pp. 1–17). Springer.
17. Hirmer, P., Wieland, M., Breitenbücher, U., & Mitschang, B. (2016). Automated sensor registration, binding and sensor data provisioning. In *Proceedings of the CAiSE'16 forum, at the 28th international conference on advanced information systems engineering* (Vol. 1612, pp. 81–88).
18. SmartOrchestra Consortium SmartOrchestra Research Project. (2016). Online, http://smartorchestra.de/en
19. IC4F Consortium IC4F Research Project. (2017). Online, https://www.ic4f.de
20. Nugent, C., Finlay, D., Davies, R., Wang, H., Zheng, H., Hallberg, J., Synnes, K., & Mulvenna, M. (2007). homeML: An open standard for the exchange of data within smart environments. In *Pervasive computing for quality of life enhancement: 5th international*

conference on smart homes and health telematics, ICOST 2007, Nara, Japan, June 21–23, 2007. Proceedings (pp. 121–129).

21. McDonald, H., Nugent, C., Hallberg, J., Finlay, D., Moore, G., & Synnes, K. (2013). The homeML suite: Shareable datasets for smart home environments. *Health And Technology, 3*(6), 177–193 (2013).

22. IEEE. (1998). IEEE standard for a smart transducer interface for sensors and actuators: Transducer to microprocessor communication protocols and transducer electronic data sheet (TEDS) formats. http://standards.ieee.org/standard/1451_2-1997.html

23. Song, E., Burns, M., Pandey, A., & Roth, T. (2019). IEEE 1451 smart sensor digital twin federation for IoT/CPS research. In *2019 IEEE sensors applications symposium (SAS)* (pp. 1–6).

24. Futek Advanced Sensor Technology, Inc (2018). Transducer electronic datasheet: Manual and programming guide. Online, www.futek.com

25. IEEE. (2010). ISO/IEC/IEEE Information technology: Smart transducer interface for sensors and actuators: Common functions, communication protocols, and transducer electronic data sheet (TEDS) formats. In *ISO/IEC/IEEE 21450:2010(E)* (pp. 1–350).

26. Conway, P., Heffernan, D., O'Mara, B., Burton, P., & Miao, T. (2000). IEEE 1451.2: An interpretation and example implementation. In *Proceedings of the 17th IEEE instrumentation and measurement technology conference (IMTC)* (Vol. 2, pp. 535–540).

27. Song, Y., & Lee, K. (2006). An implementation of the proposed IEEE 1451.0 and 1451.5 Standards. In *Proceedings of the sensors applications symposium*.

28. Cherian, A., Wobschall, D., & Sheikholeslami, M. (2017). An IoT interface for industrial analog sensor with IEEE 21451 protocol. In *Proceedings of the ieee sensors applications symposium (SAS)* (pp. 1–5).

29. Bermudez-Edo, M., Elsaleh, T., Barnaghi, P., & Taylor, K. (2017). IoT-lite: A lightweight semantic model for the internet of things and its use with dynamic semantics. *Personal And Ubiquitous Computing, 21*(6), 475–487.

30. Elsaleh, T., Enshaeifar, S., Rezvani, R., Acton, S., Janeiko, V., & Bermudez-Edo, M. (2020). IoT-stream: A lightweight ontology for internet of things data streams and its use with data analytics and event detection services. *Sensors, 20*, 953.

31. Elsaleh, T., Bermudez-Edo, M., Enshaeifar, S., Acton, S., Rezvani, R., & Barnaghi, P. (2019). IoT-stream: A lightweight ontology for internet of things data streams. In *2019 Global IoT summit (GIoTS)* (pp. 1–6).

32. Open Connectivity Foundation IoT Management and Control. (2013). Online, https://openconnectivity.org/developer/specifications/upnp-resources/upnp/iot-management-and-control1-2

33. Open Connectivity Foundation (2017). OCF architecture overview. Online, https://openconnectivity.org/business/

34. Open Connectivity Foundation IoTivity. (2017). Online, https://www.iotivity.org

35. Seydoux, N., Drira, K., Hernandez, N., & Monteil, T. (2016). IoT-O, a core-domain IoT ontology to represent connected devices networks. In *Knowledge engineering and knowledge management* (pp. 561–576). Springer.

36. Alaya, M., Medjiah, S., Monteil, T., & Drira, K. (2015). Toward semantic interoperability in oneM2M architecture. *IEEE Communications Magazine, 53*, 35–41.

37. OneM2M Partners oneM2M Base Ontology. (2018). http://www.onem2m.org/technical/latest-drafts

38. Li, W., Tropea, G., Abid, A., Detti, A., & Le Gall, F. (2019). Review of standard ontologies for the web of things. In *2019 global IoT summit (GIoTS)* (pp. 1–6).

39. OPC Foundation. (2017). OPC unified architecture specification. Part 5: Information model. https://reference.opcfoundation.org/v104/Core/docs/Part5/

40. Grüner, S., Pfrommer, J., & Palm, F. (2016). RESTful industrial communication with OPC UA. *IEEE Transactions on Industrial Informatics, 12*(10), 1832–1841.

41. OPC Foundation. (2019). OPC UA architecture overview. Online, https://opcfoundation.org/wp-content/uploads/2019/09/UA-Architecture.png

42. Jennings, C., Arkko, J., & Shelby, Z. (2012). Media types for sensor markup language (SENML). https://tools.ietf.org/html/draft-jennings-senml-10
43. Jennings, C., Shelby, Z., Arkko, J., Keranen, A., & Bormann, C. (2018). *Sensor measurement lists (SenML)*. Internet Engineering Steering Group (IESG).
44. Su, X., Zhang, H., Riekki, J., Keränen, A., Nurminen, J., & Du, L. (2014). Connecting IoT sensors to knowledge-based systems by transforming SenML to RDF. *Procedia Computer Science, 32*, 215–222. http://www.sciencedirect.com/science/article/pii/S1877050914006176. *The 5th international conference on ambient systems, networks and technologies (ANT-2014), the 4th international conference on sustainable energy information technology (SEIT-2014)*.
45. McKee, L. (2003). *SensorML structural overview*. Online, https://qtxasset.com/files/sensorsmag/nodes/2003/967/fig1.gif
46. Compton, M., Barnaghi, P., Bermudez, L., García-Castro, R., Corcho, O., Cox, S., Graybeal, J., Hauswirth, M., Henson, C., Herzog, A., Huang, V., Janowicz, K., Kelsey, W., Le Phuoc, D., Lefort, L., Leggieri, M., Neuhaus, H., Nikolov, A., Page, K., Passant, A., Sheth, A., & Taylor, K. (2012). The SSN ontology of the W3C semantic sensor network incubator group. *Web Semantics: Science, Services And Agents On The World Wide Web, 17*, 25–32.
47. Hasan, S., Curry, E., Banduk, M., & O'Riain, S. (2011). Toward situation awareness for the semantic sensor web: Complex event processing with dynamic linked data enrichment. In *Proceedings of the 4th international workshop on semantic sensor networks* (Vol. 839, pp. 60–72).
48. Janowicz, K., Haller, A., Cox, S., Le Phuoc, D., & Lefrançois, M. (2019). SOSA: A lightweight ontology for sensors, observations, samples, and actuators. *Journal Of Web Semantics, 56*, 1–10. http://www.sciencedirect.com/science/article/pii/S1570826818300295
49. Eclipse Foundation. (2017). Eclipse Vorto architecture. Online, https://www.eclipse.org/community/eclipse%5C_newsletter/2017/march/images/eclipsevorto.jpg
50. Eclipse Vorto. (2017). Online, https://github.com/eclipse/vorto, https://www.eclipse.org/vorto
51. March, S., & Scudder, G. (2017). Predictive maintenance: Strategic use of IT in manufacturing organizations. *Information Systems Frontiers*, 1–15.
52. Bauer, M., Bui, N., De Loof, J., Magerkurth, C., Nettsträter, A., Stefa, J., & Walewski, J. (2013). IoT reference model. In *Enabling things to talk: designing IoT solutions with the IoT architectural reference model* (pp. 113–162).
53. Wobschall, D. (2002). An implementation of IEEE 1451 NCAP for internet access of serial port-based sensors. In *2nd ISA/IEEE sensors for industry conference* (pp. 157–160).
54. Gubbi, J., Buyya, R., Marusic, S., & Palaniswami, M. (2013). Internet of things (IoT): A vision, architectural elements, and future directions. *Future Generation Computer Systems, 29*, 1645–1660.
55. Compton, M., Henson, C., Lefort, L., Neuhaus, H., & Sheth, A. (2009). A survey of the semantic specification of sensors. In *Proceedings of the 2nd international conference on semantic sensor networks* (Vol. 522, pp. 17–32).
56. Avancha, S., Patel, C. & Joshi, A. Ontology-driven adaptive sensor networks. In *The first annual international conference on mobile and ubiquitous systems: Networking and services, 2004 (MOBIQUITOUS 2004)* (pp. 194–202).
57. Matheus, C., Tribble, D., Kokar, M., Ceruti, M., & McGirr, S. (2006). *Towards a formal pedigree ontology for level-one sensor fusion*. Versatile Information Systems Inc.
58. Eid, M., Liscano, R., & Saddik, A. (2007). A universal ontology for sensor networks data. In *2007 IEEE international conference on computational intelligence for measurement systems and applications* (pp. 59–62).
59. Gyrard, A., Bonnet, C., Boudaoud, K., & Serrano, M. (2016). LOV4IoT: A second life for ontology-based domain knowledge to build semantic web of things applications. In *2016 IEEE 4th international conference on future internet of things and cloud (FiCloud)* (pp. 254–261).
60. Chen, C., & Helal, S. (2008). Sifting through the jungle of sensor standards. *IEEE Pervasive Computing, 7*(10), 84–88.

61. Darmois, E., Elloumi, O., Guillemin, P., & Moretto, P. (2012). IoT standards–state-of-the-art analysis. In *Digitising the industry internet of things connecting the physical, digital and virtual worlds.*
62. Grangel-Gonzälez, I., Baptista, P., Halilaj, L., Lohmann, S., Vidal, M., Mader, C., & Auer, S. (2017). The industry 4.0 standards landscape from a semantic integration perspective. In *IEEE 22nd international conference on emerging technologies and factory automation (ETFA).*
63. Zigbee Alliance Dotdot. (2019). https://zigbeealliance.org/solution/dotdot
64. Dumas, M., Rosa, M., Mendling, J., & Reijers, H. (2018). *Fundamentals of business process management* (2nd ed.). Springer. https://doi.org/10.1007/978-3-662-56509-4
65. Silva, A., Hirmer, P., Breitenbücher, U., Kopp, O., & Mitschang, B. (2018). TDLIoT: A topic description language for the internet of things. In *Proceedings of the international conference on web engineering (ICWE)* (pp. 333–348).
66. Chen, P. (1976). The entity-relationship model: Toward a unified view of data. *ACM Transaction on Database System, 1,* 9–36.
67. Grangel-González, I., Halilaj, L., Coskun, G., Auer, S., Collarana, D., & Hoffmeister, M. (2016). Towards a semantic administrative shell for industry 4.0 components. In *Proceding of the 10th international conference on semantic computing (ICSC)* (pp. 230–237).
68. HomeAssistant (2022). *Home Assistant.* Online, https://home-assistant.io/
69. Apache CouchDB NoSQL Database (2022). Online, http://couchdb.apache.org/
70. Pietzuch, P., Eyers, D., Kounev, S., & Shand, B. (2007). Towards a common API for publish/subscribe. In *Proceedings of the 2007 inaugural international conference on distributed event-based systems (DEBS)* (pp. 152–157).
71. Dai, C., & Wang, Z. (2010). A flexible extension of WSDL to describe non-functional attributes. In *2nd international conference on e-business and information system security* (pp. 1–4).
72. Weerawarana, S., Curbera, F., Leymann, F., Storey, T., & Ferguson, D. (2005). *Web services platform architecture: SOAP, WSDL, WS-Policy, WS-addressing, WS-BPEL, WS-reliable messaging and more.* Prentice Hall.
73. Papazoglou, M. (2003). Service-oriented computing: concepts, characteristics and directions. In *Proceedings of the 4th international conference on web information systems engineering (WISE)* (pp. 3–12).
74. Christensen, E., Curbera, F., Meredith, G., & Weerawarana, S. (2001). *Others web services description language (WSDL) 1.1.* (Citeseer, 2001). https://www.w3.org/TR/2001/NOTE-wsdl-20010315
75. Adams, P., Easton, P., Johnson, E., Merrick, R. & Philips, M. (2012). *SOAP over Java message service 1.0.* (online, 2012). https://www.w3.org/TR/soapjms/
76. Jimenez, J., Koster, M., & Tschofenig, H. (2016) IPSO smart objects. In *Proceedings of the IOT semantic interoperability workshop.*
77. Bormann, C., Castellani, A., & Shelby, Z. (2012). CoAP: An application protocol for billions of tiny internet nodes. *IEEE Internet Computing, 16*(3), 62–67.
78. Alliance, O.M. (2013). Lightweight machine to machine technical specification. *Technical specification OMA-TS-LightweightM2M-V1.* https://www.openmobilealliance.org/release/LightweightM2M/V1_1_1-20190617-A/OMA-TS-LightweightM2M_Core-V1_1_1-20190617-A.pdf
79. Kearney, K., & Torelli, F. (2011). The SLA model. *Service Level Agreements For Cloud Computing* (pp. 43–67). Springer.
80. Hüffmeyer, M., Hirmer, P., Mitschang, B., Schreier, U., & Wieland, M. (2017). SitAC: A system for situation-aware access control: Controlling access to sensor data. In *Proceedings of the 3rd international conference on information systems security and privacy* (Vol. 1).
81. McEwen, A., & Cassimally, H. (2013). *Designing the internet of things.* Wiley Publishing.
82. Hunkeler, U., Truong, H., & Stanford-Clark, A. (2008). MQTT-S: A publish/subscribe protocol for wireless sensor networks. In *2008 3rd international conference on communication systems software and middleware and workshops (COMSWARE '08)* (pp. 791–798).

83. Hunkeler, U., Truong, H., & Stanford-Clark, A. (2008). MQTT-S: A publish/subscribe protocol for wireless sensor networks. In *2008 3rd international conference on communication systems software and middleware and workshops (COMSWARE'08)* (pp. 791–798).

84. Del Gaudio, D., & Hirmer, P. (2019). A lightweight messaging engine for decentralized data processing in the Internet of Things. *SICS Software-Intensive Cyber-Physical Systems, 35*, 39–48 (2019). https://doi.org/10.1007/s00450-019-00410-z

85. Meunier, R. (1995). The pipes and filters architecture. In *Pattern languages of program design* (pp. 427–440). ACM.

86. Silva, A., Breitenbücher, U., Hirmer, P., Képes, K., Kopp, O., Leymann, F., Mitschang, B., & Steinke, R. (2017). Internet of things out of the box: Using TOSCA for automating the deployment of iot environments. In *Proceedings of the 7th international conference on cloud computing and services science (CLOSER)* (pp. 358–367).

87. Silva, A. et al. (2017). Customization and provisioning of complex event processing using TOSCA. *Computer Science - Research And Development, 33*, 1–11.

88. OASIS. (2013). *Topology and orchestration specification for cloud applications.* Advancing Open Standards for the Information Society. http://docs.oasis-open.org/tosca/TOSCA/v1.0/os/TOSCA-v1.0-os.pdf

89. Breitenbücher, U., Binz, T., Képes, K., Kopp, O., Leymann, F., & Wettinger, J. (2014). Combining declarative and imperative cloud application provisioning based on TOSCA. In *Proceedings of the IEEE international conference on cloud engineering (IC2E)* (pp. 87–96). http://www2.informatik.uni-stuttgart.de/cgi-bin/NCSTRL/NCSTRL%5C_view.pl?id=INPROC-2014--21%5C&engl=0

90. Bormann, C., Castellani, A., & Shelby, Z. (2012) Coap: An application protocol for billions of tiny internet nodes. *IEEE Internet Computing, 16*, 62–67.

91. Box, D., Ehnebuske, D., Kakivaya, G., Layman, A., Mendelsohn, N., Nielsen, H., Thatte, S., & Winer, D. (2000). *Simple object access protocol (SOAP) 1.1.*

92. Tanganelli, G., Vallati, C., & Mingozzi, E. (2015). CoAPthon: Easy development of CoAP-based IoT applications with Python. In *2015 IEEE 2nd world forum on internet of things (WF-IoT)* (pp. 63–68).

93. Mormul, M., Hirmer, P., Stach, C., & Mitschang, B. (2020) Avoiding vendor-lockin in cloud monitoring using generic agent templates. In *Business information systems - 23rd international conference, BIS 2020, Colorado Springs, CO, USA, June 8–10, 2020, Proceedings* (Vol. 389, pp. 367–378). https://doi.org/10.1007/978-3-030-53337-3%5C_27

94. InfluxData Telegraf. (2019). https://www.influxdata.com/time-series-platform/telegraf/

95. Elastic (2019). *Search B.V. beats.* https://www.elastic.co.de/products/beats

96. Ward, J., & Barker, A. (2014). Observing the clouds: A survey and taxonomy of cloud monitoring. *Journal Of Cloud Computing, 3*, 24.

97. Taherizadeh, S., Jones, A., Taylor, I., Zhao, Z., & Stankovski, V. (2018). Monitoring self-adaptive applications within edge computing frameworks: A state-of-the-art review. *Journal Of Systems And Software, 136*, 19–38.

98. HashiCorp. (2019). *Vagrant.* https://www.vagrantup.com/

99. Docker, Inc. (2019). *Docker.* https://www.docker.com/

100. Splunk, Inc. (2019). *Splunk.* https://www.splunk.com/

101. Opentosca. (2019). *University of Stuttgart OpenTOSCA.* https://www.opentosca.org/

102. Eclipse. (2019). *Winery.* https://eclipse.github.io/winery/

103. Breitenbücher, U., Binz, T., Kopp, O., & Leymann, F. (2014). Vinothek: A self-service portal for TOSCA. In *Proceedings of the 6th central-European workshop on services and their composition (ZEUS 2014)* (Vol. 1140, 69–72).

104. Prasad, P., & Bhalla, V. (2018). *Use this 4-step approach to architect your IT monitoring strategy.* https://www.gartner.com/en/documents/3882275/use-this-4-step-approach-to-architect-your-it-monitoring

105. Falkenthal, M., Barzen, J., Breitenbücher, U., Fehling, C., & Leymann, F. (2014). From pattern languages to solution implementations. In *Proceedings of the sixth international conference on pervasive patterns and applications (PATTERNS* (pp. 12–21).

106. Eilam, T. et al. (2011) pattern-based composite application deployment. In *Proceedings of the 12th IFIP/IEEE international symposium on integrated network management, IM 2011, Dublin, Ireland, 23–27 May 2011* (pp. 217–224).
107. Künzle, V. et al. (2011). PHILharmonicFlows: Towards a framework for object-aware process management. *Journal Of Software Maintenance And Evolution: Research And Practice, 23*(4), 205–244.
108. Cohn, D. et al. (2009). Business artifacts: A data-centric approach to modeling business operations and processes. In *Bulletin of the IEEE computer society technical committee on data engineering.*
109. Sun, Y. et al. (2014). Modeling data for business processes. In *Proceedings of the 30th IEEE international conference on data engineering (ICDE), Chicago, USA.*
110. Reimann, P., Schwarz, H., & Mitschang, B. (2014). A pattern approach to conquer the data complexity in simulation workflow design. *OTM confederated international conferences "on the move to meaningful internet systems" - 22nd international conference on cooperative information systems (CoopIS 2014)* (pp. 21–38).
111. Hirmer, P., Wieland, M., Schwarz, H., Mitschang, B., Breitenbücher, U., Sáez, S., & Leymann, F. (2016). Situation recognition and handling based on executing situation templates and situation-aware workflows. *Computing, 99*(2), 1–19.
112. Del Gaudio, D., Reichel, M., & Hirmer, P. (2020). A life cycle method for device management in dynamic iot environments. In *Proceedings of the 5th international conference on internet of things, big data and security (IoTBDS)* (Vol. 1, pp. 46–56).
113. Del Gaudio, D., & Hirmer, P. (2020). Seamless integration of devices in industry 4.0 environments. *Internet Of Things, 12,* 100321. https://www.sciencedirect.com/science/article/pii/S2542660520301529
114. Lazarescu, M. (2013). Design of a WSN platform for long-term environmental monitoring for IoT applications. *IEEE Journal On Emerging And Selected Topics In Circuits And Systems, 3,* 45–54.
115. OASIS. (2013). *TOSCA primer.* Online, http://docs.oasis-open.org/tosca/tosca-primer/v1.0/cnd01/tosca-primer-v1.0-cnd01.pdf
116. Binz, T., Breitenbücher, U., Kopp, O., & Leymann, F. (2014). TOSCA: Portable automated deployment and management of cloud applications. *Advanced Web Services,* 527–549.
117. Seeger, J., Deshmukh, A. R., Sarafov, V., & Bröring, A. (2019). Dynamic IoT choreographies. *IEEE Pervasive Computing, 18,* 19–27.
118. Peltz, C. (2003). Web services orchestration and choreography. *Computer, 36,* 46–52.
119. Silva, A., Hirmer, P., Schneider, J., Ulusal, S., & Tavares Frigo, M. (2020). MBP: Not just an IoT platform. In *Proceedings of the 18th annual IEEE international conference on pervasive computing and communications.*
120. Silva, A., Hirmer, P., & Mitschang, B. (2019). Model-based operator placement for data processing in IoT environments. In *2019 IEEE international conference on smart computing (SMARTCOMP)* (pp. 439–443).
121. Kapitanova, K., Hoque, E., Stankovic, J., Whitehouse, K., & Son, S. (2012). Being SMART about failures: Assessing repairs in SMART homes. In *Proceedings of the 2012 ACM conference on ubiquitous computing* (pp. 51–60). http://doi.acm.org/10.1145/2370216.2370225
122. Kodeswaran, P., Kokku, R., Sen, S., & Srivatsa, M. (2016). Idea: A system for efficient failure management in smart IoT environments. In *Proceedings of the 14th annual international conference on mobile systems, applications, and services* (pp. 43–56). http://doi.acm.org/10.1145/2906388.2906406
123. Datta, S., Da Costa, R., & Bonnet, C. (2015). Resource discovery in internet of things: Current trends and future standardization aspects. In *2015 IEEE 2nd world forum on internet of things (WF-IoT)* (pp. 542–547).
124. Bermudez-Edo, M., Elsaleh, T., Barnaghi, P., & Taylor, K. IoT-lite: A lightweight semantic model for the internet of things. In *2016 international IEEE conferences on ubiquitous intelligence & computing, advanced and trusted computing, scalable computing and communications, cloud and big data computing, internet of people, and smart world congress (UIC/ATC/ScalCom/CBDCom/IoP/SmartWorld)* (pp. 90–97).

125. Fredj, S., Boussard, M., Kofman, D., & Noirie, L. (2014). Efficient semantic-based IoT service discovery mechanism for dynamic environments. In *2014 IEEE 25th annual international symposium on personal, indoor, and mobile radio communication (PIMRC)* (pp. 2088–2092).

126. Shelby, Z., Hartke, K., & Bormann, C. (2014). The constrained application protocol (CoAP). *RFC.* **7252** (pp. 1–112).

127. Shelby, Z., Krco, S. & Bormann, C. (2014). *CoRE resource directory; draft-ietf-core-resource-directory-02.* (November, 2014). https://core-wg.github.io/resource-directory/draft-ietf-core-resource-directory.html

128. Cirani, S., Davoli, L., Ferrari, G., Léone, R., Medagliani, P., Picone, M., & Veltri, L. (2014). A scalable and self-configuring architecture for service discovery in the internet of things. *IEEE Internet Of Things Journal, 1*, 508–521.

129. Sciullo, L., Aguzzi, C., Di Felice, M., & Cinotti, T. (2019). WoT store: Enabling things and applications discovery for the W3C web of things. In *2019 16th IEEE annual consumer communications and networking conference, CCNC 2019.*

130. Kovatsch, M., Lanter, M., & Shelby, Z. (2014). Californium: Scalable cloud services for the internet of things with coap. In *2014 international conference on the internet of things (IOT)* (pp. 1–6).

131. Sohal, A., Sandhu, R., Sood, S., & Chang, V. (2018). A cybersecurity framework to identify malicious edge device in fog computing and cloud-of-things environments. *Computers And Security, 74*, 340–354.

132. Kuo, C., Chi, P., Chang, V., & Lei, C. (2018). SFaaS: Keeping an eye on IoT fusion environment with security fusion as a service. *Future Generation Computer Systems, 86*, 1424–1436. http://www.sciencedirect.com/science/article/pii/S0167739X17324834

133. Chang, V., Abdel-Basset, M., & Ramachandran, M. (2019). Towards a reuse strategic decision pattern framework – from theories to practices. *Information Systems Frontiers, 21*, 27–44.

134. Kaivonen, S., & Ngai, E. (2020). Real-time air pollution monitoring with sensors on city bus. *Digital Communications And Networks, 6*, 23–30. http://www.sciencedirect.com/science/article/pii/S2352864818302475

Chapter 6
Discussion

6.1 Distribution/Decentralization

Our first challenge was the high distribution of devices, sensors, actuators, as well as edge, fog, and backend cloud environments, in IoT systems. This distribution, furthermore, leads to decentralized environments that are much more difficult to control and manage.

The introduced models can help in gaining control of highly distributed systems by giving a good overview of the available hardware and software components that are being used. Using *IoT environment models* to build digital twins, it can be seen at all times which hardware components, i.e., devices, sensors, and actuators, are installed at which location and how they are interconnected. If a device fails or a new device is added, this model can be updated using the adaptation approach introduced in Sect. 5.9. By doing so, it can be ensured that the IoT environment model is kept synchronized with the physical environment at all times. The physical setup of such highly distributed environments can be supported by the business process based approach as introduced by Frigo et al. [1].

In addition, when it comes to software deployment and installation, the TOSCA standard can help in automating this process, since manual deployment becomes very cumbersome in such highly distributed environments. Once a catalog of available Cloud Service Archives (CSARs) is created, a TOSCA engine is able to connect to each device, edge, fog, or backend cloud, and deploy, install and configure software onto it. Graphical TOSCA topology models can help in maintaining an overview of the software to be deployed and can also serve documentation purposes after deployment so that it is clear which software component is running on which device.

Finally, using the approach of Mormul et al. [2], as introduced in Sect. 5.8, monitoring in decentralized environments can be conducted using Generic Agent Templates. Furthermore, using the Messaging Engine introduced by Del Gaudio et

© The Author(s), under exclusive license to Springer Nature Switzerland AG 2023
P. Hirmer, *Model-Based Approaches to the Internet of Things*,
https://doi.org/10.1007/978-3-031-18884-8_6

al. [3], communication in decentralized environments is enabled without the need for a central component.

Overall, the introduced models mostly focus on coping with the large distribution in IoT environments and the complexity that comes with it. By offering abstraction throughout the physical and digital layers, management and control of complex IoT systems can be eased.

6.2 Heterogeneity

Another challenge was the large degree of heterogeneity in the Internet of Things. Not only devices, sensors and actuators differ highly in regard to their capabilities and limitations but also a large variety of communication protocols and paradigms as well as standards exist for the IoT.

In order to cope with the high heterogeneity in the IoT, model based approaches can help by providing abstraction and a better overview. We introduced the IoT Toolbox by Frigo et al. [1], containing modular building blocks of the IoT, concerning hardware and software components. Collecting these building blocks in a toolbox, allows browsing and corresponding recommendations based on a set of requirements of an IoT application. Thus, IoT application developers do not need to know every available hardware or software component, standard, or protocol. They only need to define the requirements they have for their application and the toolbox can make according recommendations. Thus, the knowledge about available technologies can be maintained by the toolbox and can be shared between different stakeholders.

6.3 Robustness/Safety

Safety is an important issue, especially when it comes to applications in which people could come to harm (e.g., smart cities, autonomous driving). Hence, it must be ensured that a failure within an IoT system does not lead to the harm of any involved entity or person.

To ensure safety and robustness of an IoT application, it is necessary to have monitoring in place and to be able to adapt to failing devices. For monitoring, we introduced the approach of Mormul et al. [2] in Sect. 5.8, which uses models called Generic Agent Templates to enable monitoring of distributed and decentralized environments. Through comprehensive monitoring, robustness can be increased by being notified of issues and failures in a timely manner.

Furthermore, we described the approach of Del Gaudio et al. [3] for automated adaptation of message exchange between devices in the IoT in case of device failures. Using this approach, IoT applications can still be kept running, even though part of the hardware infrastructure might fail.

Of course, the mechanisms for monitoring and adaptation still need to be implemented depending on use cases and scenarios, however, through the model based abstraction, an overview of the physical and digital layers can be given that allows identifying critical areas or components in the IoT environment where monitoring needs to be in place.

6.4 Privacy

An important issue is privacy, especially when it comes to sensitive person-related data. In general, there is a high demand for protection and anonymization of personal data. Even though, privacy is not the focus in this book, the model based approaches can still help into ensuring a certain degree of privacy by design.

First, by defining privacy as a requirement for the IoT application, the IoT toolbox can provide only software components that comply with existing privacy laws or that have agreements and SLAs in place to regulate certain privacy issues. Furthermore, in the introduced data processing model (cf. Sect. 5.5.2), there could be data processing steps in place to provide anonymization of the data in order to make sure that personal data is not handed to an unauthorized entity.

6.5 Security

Security is an issue that is not only important in IoT applications but becomes more of a challenge since IoT environments are highly distributed and many IoT devices are not equipped with a sufficient degree of security-preserving measures. Hence, it is necessary to ensure security of devices during data transfer as well as for stored data.

Similar to defining privacy requirements for the toolbox, corresponding security requirements can be defined as well. By doing so, only secure communication channels (e.g., using TLS), databases that allow encryption, components that require secure passwords, and so on, will be recommended by the toolbox. This can make sure that security requirements are considered by design of the application. In addition, libraries for encryption and decryption can be recommended as software modules to be used in the application. Especially in security critical applications, this can also have influence on the hardware components to be recommended by the toolbox. For secure key storage, for example, special hardware exists that maximizes security. Furthermore, for in-transit security, secure communication channels could also require special hardware to be recommended by the toolbox.

6.6   Efficiency/Real-Time Capabilities

In fast-paced scenarios, such as autonomous driving, efficiency and real-time capabilities are important, especially regarding the communication between different IoT devices. By defining efficiency as a given requirement for our introduced toolbox, it can be ensured that only real-time capable communication channels, hardware components, and corresponding operating systems are recommended. This can make sure that real-time capabilities are considered during runtime. Furthermore, even though the corresponding hardware and software is in place, the overhead, for example, caused by monitoring agents, during runtime still needs to be kept to a minimum to ensure that the real-time requirements are not violated. For monitoring, the introduced Generic Agent Templates could then, for example, be mapped onto real-time capable monitoring agent implementations and only for the time-critical components. For other components in the IoT system without strict real-time requirements, the Agent Templates could be mapped onto slower but more robust agents.

6.7   Energy Consumption

Finally, energy consumption is important to consider since IoT devices are usually wireless and do not possess a hardwired power connection. Thus, there need to be techniques in place to minimize energy consumption. We do not provide any specific means in this book to cope with improving energy consumption, however, the toolbox can still only recommend devices that are able to go into sleep or standby mode as well as software components that can cope with such mechanisms.

Overall, we showed in this book how model based approaches can help in developing IoT applications and how the aforementioned challenges can be tackled throughout the whole life cycle of an IoT application.

References

1. Frigo, M., Hirmer, P., Silva, A., & Thom, L. (2020). A toolbox for the internet of things - easing the setup of IoT applications. In *ER forum, demo and posters 2020 co-located with 39th international conference on conceptual modeling (ER 2020), Vienna, Austria, November 3–6, 2020* (Vol. 2716, pp. 87–100). http://ceur-ws.org/Vol-2716/paper7.pdf
2. Mormul, M., Hirmer, P., Stach, C., & Mitschang, B. (2020). Avoiding vendor-lockin in cloud monitoring using generic agent templates. In *Business information systems - 23rd international conference, BIS 2020, Colorado Springs, CO, USA, June 8–10, 2020, Proceedings* (Vol. 389, pp. 367–378). https://doi.org/10.1007/978-3-030-53337-3%5C_27
3. Del Gaudio, D., & Hirmer, P. (2019). A lightweight messaging engine for decentralized data processing in the Internet of Things. *SICS Software-Intensive Cyber-Physical Systems, 35*, 39–48. https://doi.org/10.1007/s00450-019-00410-z

Chapter 7
Conclusion and Summary

This book introduces different model based approaches throughout the lifecycle of an IoT application, which have been developed within my own research or within my research group. Many of these approaches were used within industry-focused research projects. Even though we aim for generic solutions, the introduced model based approaches will be further extended in the future to optimize them or to further adapt to new technologies, protocols, and standards.

We first introduced the lifecycle of an IoT application as depicted in Fig. 7.1. This life cycle serves as foundation for all introduced approaches in this book. The method itself can be roughly divided into steps concerning physical hardware components and steps concerning software components as well as software operation. What separates IoT applications from non-IoT applications is the focus on the IoT hardware, which is typically heterogeneous, distributed, and resource-limited. By combining this infrastructure with more powerful edge, fog and backend cloud environments, new kinds of applications can be introduced that make people's lives easier throughout a large variety of different domains, for example, Smart Cities, Smart Homes, Smart Offices, or Smart Factories, minimizing physical labor by increasing the amount of automatizing.

But not only the hardware selection and installation is different in IoT applications, also the software needs to be developed differently in contrast to traditional software applications that are oftentimes running on single machines. Since the nature of IoT applications is very distributed, new ways of communication between the distributed software components need to be introduced, especially focusing on messaging and publish-subscribe based data exchanged. Especially the latter is important since data is oftentimes originating from sensors that measure data regularly or irregularly. In this manner, data consumer applications can be notified once new data arrives and do not need to poll for data, which would lead to a decrease in efficiency and an increase in network traffic.

In order to define how messages are exchanged in IoT applications, we described the Topic Description Language for IoT Applications (TDLIoT), which works

© The Author(s), under exclusive license to Springer Nature Switzerland AG 2023
P. Hirmer, *Model-Based Approaches to the Internet of Things*,
https://doi.org/10.1007/978-3-031-18884-8_7

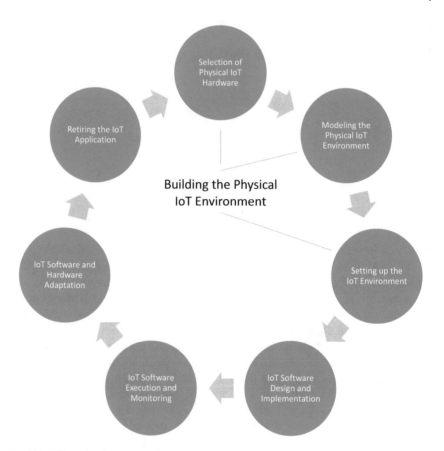

Fig. 7.1 Life cycle of an IoT application

similar to service descriptions in Service Oriented Architectures. By creating a TDLIoT description, it can be defined which data is provided by a specific topic and how the data can be accessed, including authentication mechanism, and data schemata. A corresponding catalog then enables browsing available topics and building modular IoT applications based on these topics, using the IoT data they provide.

Based on this, IoT applications can be defined using the introduced building blocks and corresponding building block implementations. By defining process models, it can then be modeled, which steps are necessary to set up the software components of an IoT application. Using, for example, the TOSCA standard, deployment and configuration can even be automated.

After the software is running, adaptation could be required if a new device enters the IoT environment or a devices leaves expectedly or unexpectedly due to a failure. To cope with such issue, we introduced a method that is able to discover leaving or newly appearing devices and seamlessly integrate them into the IoT application.

The final step is then the retirement of the IoT application, which requires termination of all running software and hardware components. To realize this, we introduced a business process model based approach, which build on the introduced TOSCA build plans and the BBI installation plans.

Printed in the United States
by Baker & Taylor Publisher Services